FILM STARS DON'T DIE
IN LIVERPOOL

PETER TURNER is a Liverpool-born actor, writer and director. He joined the National Youth Theatre aged sixteen, working extensively in theatre, film and television. Known for his parts in *The Krays*, *The Comeback* and *Spearhead*, he was selected for the Carlton's Screenwriters' Course in 1993.

PETER TURNER

FILM STARS DON'T DIE
IN LIVERPOOL

A True Story

PAN BOOKS

First published 1986 by Chatto and Windus

Published in 1988 by Penguin Books

This paperback edition published 2016 by Pan Books
an imprint of Pan Macmillan
20 New Wharf Road, London N1 9RR
Associated companies throughout the world
www.panmacmillan.com

ISBN 978-1-5098-1821-1

1 3 5 7 9 8 6 4 2

A CIP catalogue record for this book is available from the British Library.

Printed and bound by CPI Group (UK) Ltd, Croydon, CR0 4YY

FILM STARS DON'T DIE
IN LIVERPOOL

I didn't know she was sick until she went to Lancaster. There had been the usual fanfare of publicity with the same slogan written on the billboards, only with the place name changed:

'The girl who can't say "No" says "Yes" to Illinois'; or 'The girl who can't say "No" says "Yes" to East Hampton.' This time it was Lancaster, England.

It was Tuesday the 29th of September. I'd heard she'd been in England for over three weeks but as yet she hadn't telephoned. I was hoping that she might. She couldn't have forgotten the number because she'd used it so many times before. Whenever I went to Liverpool to stay with my family she'd usually phone.

'Peter, hello,' – her voice was unmistakable – 'it's Gloria.' Then she'd add, 'Guess where I am?' It was always Lime Street Station.

For me, this stay in Liverpool was special. It was the first time that I'd been asked to work at the theatre in my hometown. The play was interesting and the offer of it came at a convenient time for my family, because my parents were preparing to set off on a trip to Australia to visit my brother, Billy. The four months they would be away coincided with the job at the Liverpool Playhouse, so I would be living at home and looking after their house while they were gone.

My parents were then in their early seventies and had just celebrated their fiftieth wedding anniversary. They had never been out of England before and had never travelled on an aeroplane. They'd never been anywhere before. They were overjoyed and apprehensive at the same time – feeling nervous about flying, delighted about seeing Billy and worried about leaving the house with only me to look after it.

My mother was particularly excited; she'd been planning and dreaming about this holiday for sixteen years. There was now just over a week to go before they were due to depart. She was getting quietly hysterical.

ONE

'It's got Manila on the tickets,' she said when I walked into the kitchen.

'Really. When did they arrive?' I said, sitting down at the table and opening up the paper wallet stuffed with airline tickets and counterfoils.

My mother didn't reply. She looked troubled and uncertain as she filled the kettle and took it over to the gas stove. Then she lit the grill and I knew she was about to cook me breakfast.

She spends most of her time in the kitchen; it's her domain and completely under her control. Anyone who enters is automatically given something to eat and drink – a habit left over from the days of bringing up her nine children, my elder brothers and sisters who, like me, had long since left home.

'Would you like bacon?'

'No thanks, Mum. I don't like to eat in the morning.' She'd been asking me the same question every day for the past six weeks.

'You could have fooled me.' She looked at me and smiled, obviously having heard me get home after two in the morning. 'Anyway, the morning's nearly the afternoon. Will you have toast?'

'Okay. All right then, Mum. I'll have toast.'

She came and sat down at the table and rested her head in her hands. I knew that she wanted to talk.

'I was never told anything about spending a night in Manila,' she frowned.

'It's probably just a stop-over,' I tried to reassure her. 'You might not leave the plane.'

'Oh, no. We're spending the night there. That's what it says. The travel agents have sent me a letter.'

I looked again through the tickets and found the letter which explained that they would be spending a night and a day in Manila on the way back from Australia.

'You're right,' I said. 'That's wonderful. They've arranged a hotel. You'll be staying the night.'

'I don't think it's wonderful.' My mother shook her head from side to side. 'I wish that woman in the travel agents would have let me know before now. I'll have to go and have a word with her about this.'

'Do you want me to phone and find out more?'

'Oh, no. I'll go in and see her,' she replied. 'Joe and Jessie are coming down in the car. We're all going into town shopping. I'll go in and see her.' She stood up from the table and started to make the toast.

It had been a very good summer, but over the last few days I felt it was coming to an end. The days were still bright but less sunny and it was beginning to get cold. The leaves were changing colour and some had already fallen off the plane tree in the back garden which leant dangerously towards the house.

'That tree looks as if it's getting worse,' I said.

4

'I know that it is, I keep on telling your father,' she said as she brought the well-done toast over to the table. 'I just hope that nothing happens to it while we're away. It could fall down. Anything might happen! I don't want to get back from Australia and find the house in ruins. It's things like that which put me off going.'

I buttered the toast and started to eat while my mother fell back into her thoughts. She sat as before, with her head resting on the palm of her left hand.

'Where exactly is Manila?' she sighed after a while.

'It's in the Philippines,' I answered.

'Oh my God. What am I going to tell your father?' she said in a sudden explosion of panic. 'He hates anything like that.'

'You're getting yourself too worked up about this journey,' I told her. 'Don't worry about it.'

'It's your father that I'm worried about. You know what he's like.'

She stood up to clear the table and just then the doorbell rang.

'It'll be Joe. Will you open the door?'

'All right. Mum. I'll go.'

It wasn't Joe. It was Jessie, his wife.

'Hi, Pete. I didn't expect to see you, I thought you'd still be in bed.' She leant towards me and lowered her voice. 'We're taking your mother for a meal and Joe wants to buy her a suitcase. It's the last chance we'll get before she goes to Australia. Why don't you come with us?'

Although it was only an ordinary weekday morning, Jessie was dressed as if for a special occasion. I supposed the reason she had on her crimplene two-piece was to show us all just how nice it looked, for she'd also made my mother one to take away on her trip. Not normally one who wears a lot of make-up, Jessie had MaxFactor'd her face, and was wearing her gold-plated watch-chain around her neck.

'You look nice,' I said. 'Where's Joe?'

'Oh, he's in the road doing something to the car.'

I looked towards the street and could see my oldest brother, dressed in his best suit, examining the engine. As I passed Jessie to walk down the path towards Joe, she called after me. 'There's the phone. Shall I get it?'

'No, it's all right. I will,' I said, and went back into the house.

When I returned to the kitchen Joe was sitting by the table reading the *Daily Mirror*, studying the racing form. Jessie was standing by the sink holding the wallet of tickets.

'You'll be staying in a luxury hotel.'

'I wouldn't like to stay in a hotel.'

'You'll be waited on hand and foot.'

'I don't want to be waited on hand and foot.'

'Well, it will be lovely to have a day in Manila,' she was trying to reason with my mother.

'No, Jessie, it won't,' my mother decreed. 'I don't want to be spending a day walking around the Philippines. I'll just want to get back home, especially after saying goodbye to Billy, I might never see him again. Who was that on the phone?' she turned to me and asked, trying to change the subject.

They all looked towards me for a reply but at first I said nothing.

'Who was on the phone?' my mother asked again.

'It . . . it was a call from Lancaster,' I replied.

'Oh, it's Gloria! It must be Gloria!' Jessie sounded delighted. 'Is she coming to stay?'

'No, Jessie. There's something wrong, I've got to go and see her right away.'

Instead of taking my mother into town, Joe and Jessie took me to Lancaster in their car.

It was a silent journey, Joe was concentrating on his driving and Jessie looked as if she was too frightened to speak because he was driving very fast; at one point I leant over from the back seat to look at the speed clock and realized that we were travelling way over the limit. I sat quietly, admiring my brother's motorway driving, but also anxious that the journey wasn't going to be a waste of his day. It had happened before that I'd been telephoned from a theatre where Gloria was appearing, asking if I could get there quickly. She sometimes got nervous before an opening night and I would be asked to do a bit of coaxing. I wondered if this was the case now.

And I remembered the time that Gloria telephoned from New York, asking me to get to her as soon as possible.

'I've had a terrible accident, Peter. I'm all alone, I can't walk. It's my legs.'

When I got to her two days later I could see that there was nothing wrong with her legs but her foot was swollen and looked a bit sore. The terrible accident turned out to be a splinter.

But as I looked out of the window of Joe's car, almost hypnotized by the colours the rain was making on the surface of the road, I went over in my mind the telephone conversation that I'd had with the person from Lancaster.

'Gloria is ill. It really is important that you get here,' he said.

'What's wrong with her?' I'd asked.

'I can't say. I think you ought to come.'

'That's going to be difficult. I have to be back in Liverpool by six-thirty to do my own show. I'm appearing in a play here.'

'Don't worry about that,' he said. 'Just come to Gloria's hotel. We'll make sure that you get back to Liverpool in time. We'll have a fast car waiting to take you.'

When we arrived in Lancaster we went straight to the hotel, where I was told that Gloria had been having pains in her stomach ever since she had arrived but she dismissed them and carried on working.

'She even travelled to Manchester on Friday night to see a play', I was told. 'Then the next day she collapsed in rehearsals and was taken to the hospital. She stayed there until Sunday. Then she left. Against the advice of the doctor she just signed herself out and came back here.'

It was a small hotel. The lounge was in the hallway and beyond it the reception area served as a dining room. Leaving Joe and Jessie standing at the desk, I followed the proprietor up a back stairway to Gloria's room.

'She's been here like this for two days now,' he told me as we arrived at the door to her room. 'It's difficult to know what to do.'

I knocked.

'Gloria, it's me,' I called. There was no reply, so I opened the door.

I couldn't see her, just an empty bed with an open suitcase on it. Then I heard the familiar American drawl.

'Peter,' she said. 'You're here.'

I opened the door wider, expecting to find her standing behind it, but realized she was lying in another bed that was up against the wall. I went in and shut the door behind me. The room was small. The curtains were half closed. It was almost dark. Except for a tangle of blonde hair, I couldn't actually see Gloria. She was completely covered by a blanket.

'Gloria,' I said. 'They've told me that you're sick.'

'Oh no, Peter. It's nothing. I fainted so they took me to the hospital. Huh,' she murmured, 'have you ever heard of such a thing?'

I walked towards her but she stopped me.

'No! Don't come close, honey. Sit on the other bed.'

I sat down next to the suitcase.

'Why didn't you tell me you were here? Why didn't you call me? I would have come sooner.'

'I've been so busy, Peter. I've been working on a play.'

'Gloria, what's wrong?' I asked. 'Let me see your face.'

'Don't look at me,' she said, but slowly pulled away the blanket.

I couldn't take my eyes off her. She was wearing old make-up and her face was thin and grey. Her hair was knotted and the brown roots showed. I had to look away.

There beside me in the suitcase were publicity photographs of her looking as one would expect; just like a glamorous Hollywood star. The photographs were from a film she'd made the previous year in Georgia. I remembered how we spent a long time together one night in the New York apartment carefully choosing the ones that were to be printed up from the contact sheet. They were some of the best recent photographs that she had had taken. Lying a few feet away in the other bed, Gloria was almost unrecognisable.

'I had gas in my stomach,' she continued. 'The doctor gave me a shot. I can't stand up. He's made me sick, Peter.'

She started to cough so I went to her and held her till she stopped.

'Don't touch my stomach, Peter, but help me sit up. Let me have some juice.'

On the table next to the bed, amongst a collection of paper towels and vitamin pills, was a jug of grape juice. I fed her through a straw. In between sips she spoke.

'Don't take me back to that hospital, Peter.'

'No, I won't,' I said. 'It's going to be okay.'

We sat on the bed together in silence until Jessie came into the room.

'Gloria. Hello. It's me.' Jessie's smile froze, she seemed uncertain what to say. 'We all travelled here together. Joe's downstairs.' She turned towards me and whispered, 'Peter, he wants to speak to you.'

'There's someone on the telephone,' Joe said when I joined him at the desk. 'He wants to have a word.'

He handed me the receiver and then he walked away.

'I'm a consultant from the hospital here. I understand that

you're a friend and so I've been asked to have a word with you.' He paused. 'I'm afraid Miss Grahame has a cancer. It's about the size of a football. She should be operated on immediately.'

'Is she going to be all right?' I asked.

'Well,' he answered, 'I'm afraid that it's quite serious.'

Everything else evaporated, only the taste of nicotine and stale breath lingered on the mouth piece.

I returned to Gloria's room.

'Everything okay?' Joe was standing just inside the doorway.

I could tell by the way he spoke that he knew what I'd just been told. I nodded my head in reply.

'Gloria –' I sat close to her on the bed – 'you need to be looked after. You can't stay here alone.'

'Are you gonna stay here with me, Peter?'

'No, not that,' I said. 'I think you should go to the hospital.'

'I'm not going to do that, Peter.' Her voice turned earnest and fearful. 'That doctor's done this to me. He doesn't like me,' she cried. 'Don't take me to that hospital. I'm gonna open in the play.'

'Gloria.' I held her hand and stopped her. 'I've just spoken to the doctor. He's told me that you're ill.'

She fell silent and started to listen.

'He wants to get you better. Then you can do the play. We all want you to do the play but we want you to get better. Then you'll be able to do the play.'

She looked round at Jessie and then at Joe until she rested her eyes upon me.

'Okay, Peter,' she said. 'Take me to Liverpool.'

'You make it sound romantic.'

'But it is. It's just gotta be.' Then she did it again. Beginning with a slow intake of breath, after which her lips began to quiver and then took shape for a passionate release of sound. 'Liverpooool,' she said. 'I'd really like to live there.'

I laughed.

'Peter,' she snapped. 'Don't be so mean.' Then she snatched hold of the shade of the table lamp and twisted it round so that the letters were facing the wall, 'I don't like people staring.'

'You wanted to come here,' I reminded her.

'Well, now I want to go home again. Fancy putting my name on a lamp.'

The practice did seem bizarre. This wasn't a place in which to be discreet but the restaurant was fun and flashy and part of the whole New York glamorous showbiz scene. Most of the tables had lamps on them, lit up, advertising the names of the famous faces who occasionally would be seen sitting there. Sometimes the wrong person would be seated beside the wrong lamp causing a lot of displeasure and confusion or, for some, absolute delight – as was the case with the two people at the next table, wide-eyed and self-conscious, sitting on either side of LIZA MINNELLI. However, sitting opposite was the real Ethel Merman, as well as her lamp, surrounded by admirers. One of them had accidentally knocked her shade askew so that the 'R' had fallen down between the ketchup and the napkins.

'Look. That's really funny,' I said. 'Somebody's knocked off her "R".'

Gloria livened up. 'That's a good idea,' she said and began pulling off the stick-on letters from around the side of her shade. Then she twisted it round into view.

'G O IA   RAHAM ', it read.

Sabotage proved to be ineffective. Just then a man with an entourage passed by the table and stopped to say hello.

'You look faabulous!' he screamed. 'Welcome back to New York.'

'Oh, thank you. Thank you.' Gloria smiled and looked seductive. Then instantly, almost automatically, she clicked her tongue against the roof of her mouth and threw her hair back, then to one side. That was her look – the 'Grahame' look.

Though some people might not distinguish her name or maybe had forgotten it, most knew her face from countless films of the 1950s, skulking up to Humphrey Bogart in *In a Lonely Place*, or mixing drinks for Lee Marvin in *The Big Heat*, before getting scalding coffee thrown at her. She was always regarded as a film actress of considerable worth. Although her best work was in little known films such as *Crossfire* and *Sudden Fear*, she received recognition for her performances in the famous ones, winning an Oscar for her part in *The Bad and the Beautiful*. She was as funny as Ado Annie in *Oklahoma!* and wise-cracking as the elephant girl in DeMille's *The Greatest Show on Earth*. Good at playing the floosie and the moll, she was the epitome of the tart with the heart.

'Peter,' she said, when the group had passed by, 'I think I'd like to go.'

We left by way of the lavatories and avoided having to go round the famous tables saying innumerable goodbyes.

'That's not a restaurant. It's an anti-restaurant,' she said and marched away.

I lit a cigarette then followed her along the street.

'Hey,' she said when I caught up with her. 'Let me take a blow.'

'You look like Lauren Bacall when you smoke,' I told her and passed the cigarette.

'Oh thanks,' she replied, then threw it in the gutter. 'Fancy being labelled on a table,' she continued. 'I feel like some kind of freak.'

We stopped when we reached 9th Avenue and waited for the night dustcarts to pass before we crossed the street. A fast shiver, almost orgasmic, vibrated my body. I was excited to be in New York.

In just over a year so much had changed dramatically. From living alone in London, working in a junk shop at the corner of the street whilst trying to find work as an actor, now I was in New York and involved in a relationship which had changed my life.

Gloria held on to my arm while we sauntered over the road to walk the few blocks down to 43rd.

Although I didn't know the city well, I recognized a very special New York night. It was quiet and it was still. The air was cool and almost smelled sweet, helped by the breezes coming across from the Hudson River.

'Look up,' I said. 'Ah, the stars are in the sky.'

'Yeah,' she muttered under her breath. 'That's where they should be, I guess.' She gave me a sultry look and strutted on ahead to the apartment block.

She always dressed the same. Mostly wearing blue jeans and black suede stilettoes, white shirt with black tie and a black cotton jacket. She didn't have many clothes; she found it difficult to choose them. She either took over other people's or wore what she was given. One night at the theatre, wearing her usual outfit, she was spotted by a man who gave her a gift of his very own fur coat – he wanted her to look like a 'movie star'.

'Oh Peter. You bastard. Don't be so horrible. Don't be so cruel!' she squealed when I crept up behind her and startled her outside the elevator.

'Okay, okay. I'm sorry. Forget it,' I said. 'Only trying to make you smile.' She sulked all the way up to the twenty-fifth floor. I had to turn away. Her petulant moods never failed to make me laugh.

I knew why she was upset but I thought that she had overreacted. It was such a silly thing. Earlier that day we'd been walking through Greenwich Village when we were stopped on the street by a man who invited us into his shop. It was called 'Ron's Then and Now'. The walls were covered in posters and photographs of film and theatre stars. He brought out a box and began to show Gloria photographs of herself from her early films.

'Look at this one, Gloria,' he enthused. 'It's from *It's a Wonderful Life*. It was taken in 1946.' Gloria looked horrified.

'No, it wasn't,' she told him. 'That's a mistake. It should be 1956.' She bought all the photographs and we quickly left.

She didn't like attention being drawn to the fact that I was more than twenty years younger than she was.

I knew that her mood would eventually warm once we were back inside, after she'd been to the bathroom to re-fresh her make-up and I'd put her favourite music on the tape machine – Elton John's 'Song for Guy'.

Gloria had spent little time in her rented apartment over the last two years. She'd been away from New York, either working in the theatre in England or filming in California. The rooms felt unlived in and had very few pieces of furniture; the bedroom had only a bed and a telephone; the living room was almost empty, but was dominated by a spectacular view – a vast panorama of the New York skyline in shadows and neon. I spent a lot of time looking out of the window, I was captivated, mesmerized by the down below, the continuous performance, the scenes, comings and goings on 42nd Street. I propped myself up against the glass.

'What's that?' I asked when she emerged and joined me at the window, looking stunning in a silk kimono.

'The Chrysler Building,' she said. 'Isn't it pretty?' Then, at last, she smiled.

The beautiful art deco building with its incredible ornate curves was prominent in the sky. We looked out onto the night.

Except for the twinkling of distant lights and the sudden glare of illuminated signs telling us how far we had to go, my journey back to Liverpool from Lancaster was unmemorable. My mind was blocked with thoughts of Gloria. I hadn't wanted to leave her behind.

'It's going to be a long journey back,' Joe had said to me at the hotel. 'I'm not going to be speeding down the motorway with Gloria like she is, lying in the back seat of the car. I'll be taking it slow. If I was you I'd take up that offer of a fast ride back so that you'll make it on time for yer play. Me and Jessie'll look after Gloria. We'll make all the arrangements to leave this hotel and take her back to me ma's. I just think you ought to get back as quick as you can.'

'Why did you bother to turn up? You could have just phoned yours in,' Geoffrey, one of the actors sneered, as I rushed through the stage door.

Old Jack, the stage manager, looked up as I passed his office. 'You've got twenty minutes!' he shouted.

I quickly went through my preparations for the night's performance. Undressing, then dressing, and gathering together personal props. The dressing room was empty except for Eric, who didn't go on until the second act. He looked up from his book and shrugged, as if to say 'Who cares?'. Then he rolled a cigarette.

Downstairs, behind the stage, Linda, playing her first part since leaving drama school, was practising her yoga in the way of Geoffrey, who was pacing back and forth going over his lines. I disappeared into the blackness of the wings, avoiding my friend Gil, the leading actress, who I knew wanted to talk. We'd normally use this time to discuss in detail everything we'd had to eat that day. But tonight I needed a few minutes alone before the start of the first act.

The play dragged on. I was anxious for it to end. When it did I left the theatre as quickly as I could.

The city was particularly quiet and empty, even for a Tuesday night. There was a gale blowing through the precinct. The wind was cutting and wet. I started across the square, through the passage that runs past Marks & Spencer, and turned the corner into Church Street, where I thought I would find a taxi. There were three of them huddled together for company with their 'For Hire' lights dimly lit. Ten minutes later I was home.

The house was in darkness, but halfway up the path I could see flickers of coloured light, reflections from the television, coming through the net curtains of the downstairs living room window.

As I took my coat off in the hall I could hear voices in the kitchen, which came to an abrupt silence the moment I opened the door. Joe, Jessie and my mother were gathered around the table.

'Oh, it's all right,' my mother said, and her serious expression relaxed. Then in a hushed voice she added, 'Shut that door. We're talking. I thought it might have been your father.'

'The last time I saw him he was asleep in front of the television,' Jessie informed.

'Good. That's all right then,' my mother decided. Then she froze her expression dramatically and listened for any noises from the living room, just to make sure. 'You know what your father's like,' she explained. 'He doesn't like talk.'

I closed the door behind me and leant against the fridge.

'Well, this is certainly a turn-up for the books,' my mother announced. 'I'm going to the other side of the world next week! I didn't expect anything like this.'

'Where's Gloria?' I asked.

'She's sleeping,' Jessie said. 'She's tired after that journey. It took a long time, didn't it, Joe?'

Joe nodded silently.

'Gloria's very sick.' My mother shook her head from side to side. 'I could see as soon as I opened the door to the girl. I've seen that look before. I know what's wrong with her.'

'Which room is she in?' I said.

'She's in the middle room.' My mother pointed to the ceiling.

The house, like a lot of the Victorian-built houses in the neighbourhood, had been converted into flats. There were three of them – the downstairs flat, the upstairs flat and the top flat. My sister Eileen and her husband had bought the house in this condition but had never reconverted it because they unexpectedly went to live abroad. So my mother and father, after living for years in a council house, were invited to move in. They welcomed the change but, without my sister there, they were confused as to which part of the house they should actually live in.

My mother preferred the downstairs flat because it was 'easier' – the kitchen was bigger than the others and the garden was useful for hanging up the washing, and provided another exit to the street. She would, however, sometimes move into the upstairs one for Christmas or Easter, or if ever she got fed up and just fancied a change. Otherwise it lay empty, except for visiting family members like myself. The top flat, the biggest, was rented out to students who were often to be heard singing Gilbert and Sullivan; they were practising for their end of term production of *The Pirates of Penzance*. The room which Gloria was in was a kind of no-man's land, halfway up the stairs, leading off a landing at the back of the house, and directly above my mother's kitchen. It was called the 'middle room'; the room where people stayed when they only came for a short time.

Gloria wasn't sleeping. She was 'thinking'. Thinking was one of her pastimes. She would often enjoy spending long periods by herself just thinking, sitting with a finger to her lips and looking serious and intense. Occasionally her eyes would light up, the finger would come away from her mouth, and she would turn her head as if to say something, but then suddenly change her mind and continue as before. Eventually her thoughts would come together and she would involve me in a discussion of some kind, usually about relationships and love.

Lying against the pillows, looking directly into the light coming from the lamp on the table next to her, she was immersed in her thoughts. I closed the door and she slowly turned her head.

'Oh, Peter,' she said when she saw it was me. 'Did I make you late for your play?'

'No, you didn't. Of course you didn't.' I sat down facing her at the bottom of the bed.

The room was big enough for two single beds with a table in between. There was also a chair, a hard-backed, straight wooden chair.

She smiled at me and pointed towards a small black hold-all leaning against the chair. I opened it and could see what she wanted; a green plastic wash-bag in which she kept her make-up.

'Oh hand me that, honey,' she said. 'It might have something I need.'

She pulled out a piece of broken mirror and winced when she took a look.

'I thought as much, I've been taken to the laundry.'

Her hair had been brushed, her face had been washed and she was wearing a flowery cotton nightdress that belonged to my mother.

I opened her suitcase onto the empty bed and started to unpack. Besides knickers and socks, there were her photographs, two pairs of jeans, a short white fur coat, a grey knitted sweater with a collar, a few white shirts, some vests, a tie and a pair of silk pyjamas. Underneath all these were her precious black suede shoes.

Gloria had problems buying shoes because she had problems with her feet. They were big. It really was difficult for her to find a decent-looking pair that would fit, so she would trudge around the shops for hours, most times in vain. The black suede stilettos came from a shop in Bond Street, I sat with her the day she bought them, trying to encourage her, while she went through almost every shoe in the shop. She was miserable and close to tears. The shoes she was wearing, her only pair, were caving in at the heel and about to fall off her feet. The shop was near to closing and the assistant was getting bored, but Gloria was determined. Finally the manager came up with the black suede stilettos. Gloria squeezed her way into them.

'I think it would rather help, madam,' the woman said sarcastically, 'if you would not wear socks while trying the shoes.'

'I don't happen to agree,' Gloria said in a perfect English accent. Then standing up and reverting to her American film star's voice she announced to the world, 'I always wear socks!'

It was a peculiar and unnecessary habit. She did wear socks, she always wore them, because she was embarrassed about the size of her feet.

'I remember when you bought these.' I held the shoes up to her. 'It was over three years ago. Not long after we'd met, I'm amazed you still have them.'

'So am I,' she sighed. 'Those shoes are so important to me, I keep on having them fixed.'

I moved up close to her and took her hand.

'I have gas in my stomach, Peter, that's all. That doctor gave me a shot. Now look what's happened. It's made me feel that I'm dying. Huh.' She faked a short laugh. 'Now isn't that stupid?'

Suddenly she started to breathe heavily and gulp and swallow.

'Burp me, Peter. Please, burp me.'

I lifted her away from the pillow and gently rubbed her back.

'Don't tell Paulette.' She squeezed my hand. 'Don't tell my kids.'

'Let me take you to a hospital,' I said.

'No, don't do that, Peter,' she whispered. 'I don't want a fuss.'

I could see the determination in her expression and knew she would not be moved.

'Are you listening to me, Peter? I don't want any fuss.'

*

'Eugh! You gave me a fright!'

I bumped into Jessie at the bottom of the stairs.

'I was just going to say goodnight to Gloria,' she said. 'I want to see if she needs anything. Me and Joe have got to go home soon, we've got to get back to the kids.'

'She needs another nightdress,' I said. 'I don't think she likes the one she's wearing. And she's asked me to get her some apricot kernels and grape juice from a health food shop.'

'Well look, Joe and I have got to go into town tomorrow because we still haven't got that suitcase for your mother, so we'll take you. Let's say we'll call for you here at about half past ten in the morning. I'll arrange it all with Joe.' She went upstairs to the middle room and I waited till she closed the door behind her.

When I entered the kitchen, Joe was sitting at the table over a bowl of hot soup. My mother was clearing up.

'There's some of that for you.' She turned away from the sink and pointed to the soup. 'I gave some to Gloria just before you got home but she could only manage a sip.' She dried her hands and sat down next to Joe. 'Now look. The thing is we've got to get Gloria to a hospital because we don't know how bad she is. She's got to be attended to properly. You can't have somebody sick without a doctor.'

'She's told me that she doesn't want to go to a hospital. She hates hospitals,' I said. 'I don't know what we can do.'

'We'll just have to persuade her to go.' My mother looked to Joe and then back to me. 'She could be in jeopardy of her life.'

'What do you think I should do, Joe?'

'I think you should phone her daughter in California,' he said.

'So do I,' my mother added. 'Someone will have to come over here quick. There might be unexpected things to deal with.'

'She asked me not to tell Paulette,' I said.

'Now look –' my mother held herself upright at the table, – 'I'm going to have to take charge over this lot. You've got to phone her daughter. That family has got to be told.'

'I know. I do know that. I'm just telling you what Gloria said to me.'

'I think that this is a terrible thing and I don't want Gloria to suffer, but I can't take the burden of it now, I just want to go to Australia.' She stood up to leave the room. 'Tell your father I've gone to bed.'

'Does he know about Manila?' I asked.

'Don't talk to me about bloody Manila. It might be that we won't be going anywhere.' She pushed open the kitchen door and bumped into Jessie in the hall.

'Eugh! That's twice tonight.' I heard Jessie say before the door slammed shut.

'How do you feel?' Joe handed me a cigarette.

'Shocked,' I think I said. 'Shocked.'

It was after one in the morning by the time my father put his head around the kitchen door.

'Hello there,' he said, and scratched the back of his head. 'I didn't hear you get back. It must be late. Your ma must have gone to bed then, has she?'

'Yes,' I said. 'She's gone to bed.'

'Joe and Jessie must have gone home then, have they?'

'Yes, Dad. They've gone home.'

'Oh well,' he yawned. 'That's me for the night then. I'll just let the dog out for a while.'

Candy appeared and trailed after him.

'Are you going to Manila?' I asked as he unbolted the back door.

'I'll go anywhere, me,' he said. 'I don't mind where I go.'

Only a few of her things were scattered about the room but it seemed as if she'd always been there. Somehow she didn't look out of place.

I stood at the end of her bed watching her breathing. When I was sure she was asleep I switched off the light but left the door open in case she called out in the night. Then I went to the upstairs flat.

The room was cold and in darkness.

I dialled Paulette's number in California – nobody answered.

I sat by the window under the light from the lamp in the street, holding the telephone, just letting it ring . . .

TWO

'Let's go and take a look at where I used to live,' Gloria said, slamming on the brakes and throwing the car into reverse.

We shot across to the other side of the road, managing to miss a truck that appeared from around the bend, and then the car stalled on a small ridge at the entrance to the drive. We slid back down onto the highway.

I panicked. I wasn't sure if I should be frightened from the left or from the right because I was in California, in a car going backwards, on the other side of the road, whichever that was, and the traffic was coming at us from every side. Suddenly we stopped. Then she accelerated. We veered back across the road, bumped up the ridge and ended safely in the driveway of a big house.

'Gloria. Why did you do that?'

'It's not my fault, Peter. It's that stupid gateway. It's at the top of a mountain!'

It was wonderful to get out of the car. I thought we were only going on a short trip but it had ended up being a three-hour journey. We'd driven to the shops in Santa Monica to buy groceries; Gloria had invited her mother and Joy, her sister, over for a meal. We took a detour through Hollywood and Beverly Hills on the way home; partly because Gloria's driving was so awful that I couldn't cope with going back on the freeway, and partly because it just seemed the best thing to do on a really beautiful day.

For the first few days of my stay in California the weather had been dreary. It was drizzly and everything looked grey. Now, the sky was a diamond; the buildings and the roads, the cars and the people all glistened. Palm trees, plants and flowers, the colours of which I'd only seen in a paintbox, were new to me. The names of the roads excited me: Sunset Boulevard, La Cienega, La Brea and Vine. Everything was enchanting, even the people. They all looked beautiful, healthy and clean, dry-cleaned and rich, very rich. Especially in Bel Air, where every other house looked like a *Beverly Hillbillies* mansion.

We were driving through Brentwood when Gloria spotted the house. It was an impressive-looking building, owned by the writer and producer Cy Howard, Gloria's third husband and father of her daughter Paulette. The marriage ended in divorce. Their union lasted for a number of years between Gloria's second marriage – to Nicholas Ray, the brilliant and innovative film director by whom Gloria had a son called Tim – and her fourth marriage to her former stepson, Nicholas Ray's son Tony Ray, by whom Gloria had two more children. It was a family of complicated relationships.

'What do you think of the house, Peter? Do you like it?' Gloria whispered quickly.

We had to peer through the protective screen of tall trees so that I could get a proper look, Gloria didn't want to be 'seen' unannounced. I almost felt that at any moment we would be set upon by a pack of hounds and taken before the master on suspicion of being vagabonds and thieves. I was reminded of a time in my childhood in Liverpool when my brothers, John and Frank, took me on one of their escapades to steal apples from the gardens of the houses where the rich people lived. Once we were discovered, and because I was the youngest and couldn't run as fast as they, I was left hanging on a wall and was the one that got caught.

'Yes. I do like it,' I whispered back. 'It's nice. Did you like living there?'

'Yeah, it was fun.' Gloria took my arm and we stood away from the trees. 'Betty and Bogey lived right over there,' she added, pointing to the mansion next door.

'That must have been incredible,' I said. 'Did you see a lot of them?'

'Oh no, not really, Peter. Not when I was married to Cy. How often do you run across the neighbours? But we used to spend a lot of time together when I was married to Nick. He and Bogey started up a film company. And I worked alongside him in *In a Lonely Place*. He taught me little tricks; "Just keep it in the shadows, Gloria," he used to say. "Let the camera come to you." I liked him. A few times he called me up.' She folded her arms and thought for a while. 'We used to go out on the boat, stuff like that. It was nice. Bogey just loved that boat.' Gloria clicked her tongue against the roof of her mouth. 'Hmm,' she winced. 'That Betty. She always looked so good.'

We sat back in the car and Gloria put her head out of the window to have a last look.

'Cy Howard just loved this place. He's so proud of it. He adored it.'

'Why did you leave?' I asked.

She thought for a while and then miraculously negotiated a three point turn.

'I guess Cy and I just wanted different things from life. Who knows?' She bumped the car back out of the difficult entrance to the driveway. 'But I'm sure glad that I got that divorce, Peter. I might have had an accident just driving home!'

The car squealed and tilted to one side as she turned the bend and careered on down the winding roads that led to the coast.

Gloria lived in a caravan. She called it a trailer. Positioned along the Pacific Coast Highway not far from Pacific Palisades, between Santa Monica and Malibu, it had a stunning view of the ocean. After living in luxury houses in exclusive parts of Beverly Hills, now Gloria much preferred the trailer. She enjoyed it as a retreat on her visits from London and New York.

'There's no way that I'll have a heart attack trying to keep up the payments,' she told me. 'I adore it. It's cheap, it's easy to keep clean and I don't have to vacuum. Peter,' she confessed, 'I've never vacuumed.'

It was small. The bedroom was at one end with the bathroom next door to it. In the middle was the living room that converted into another bedroom, and at the front end, overlooking the ocean, was the kitchen. Built on the side was a wooden cabin used as a day room and at the back was a little garden where Gloria grew tomatoes and flowers. The swimming pool, also used by other residents of the trailer park, was outside the kitchen window. I thought it idyllic.

Her mother and Joy were sitting in the day room which was cool and shaded from the sun. Whereas Gloria genuinely looked a lot younger than her actual age, I suspected that Joy probably looked a lot older than hers. Although they were both tall, Joy was a bigger woman than Gloria, with a darker complexion, a deeper voice and a well-worn look. She didn't wear make-up. She was plainly dressed. It was difficult to believe that they were sisters.

'Well hello, Peter.' Joy stood up to greet me. 'I've been looking forward to making your acquaintance. Mother and I are just having tea and English muffins. Come and join us.'

Mother wasn't quite sure who I was but smiled and said, 'Hello, dear.'

She was well over eighty. Wearing a mauve twin-set and a row of beads, with her hair waved and rouge on her cheeks, she reminded me of a little bird, a little operatic songbird. Her voice was high-pitched and seemed to demand great effort. Her accent changed in varying degrees from a lowland Scottish to a proper English pronunciation, but sometimes fell into West Coast American slang.

'Have you ever come across my friend Violet Fairbrother back there in England?' she said.

'No,' I replied. 'I've never come across her.' I had no idea who Violet was.

'Oh not now, Mother dear,' Joy interrupted. 'Peter doesn't want to know about Violet now. Let's ask him later.'

Mother wasn't easily put off. While Gloria prepared a meal of carrot juice, baked potatoes and salad, I sat enthralled while Mother unravelled some of her history and family background.

Mother was called Jean MacDougall. She was born in Scotland but moved to England in her teens where she studied acting at the Royal Academy of Dramatic Art. Along with her best friend, Violet Fairbrother, she was, she told me, a star pupil and went on to play Puck at a London theatre before being asked to join the Benson Players, a forerunner of the Royal Shakespeare Company, at Stratford-upon-Avon.

When she married Gloria's father, Michael Hallward, she gave up the theatre and they emigrated to Canada, where Joy was born. The family then moved to Pasadena, California, where Jean gave birth to Gloria. When she was divorced by Michael Hallward, Jean started teaching acting and elocution at her home to keep the family going. Gloria was her 'star' pupil and she was determined that her daughter would become an actress. One of Gloria's first acting parts was as 'Glamorous Gloria' in a high school play. Jean's encouragement and determination for her daughter to succeed were rewarded when Gloria, after leaving high school, was asked to play Dodie in *Goodnight Ladies* at the Blackstone Theatre in Chicago.

Mother chaperoned her daughter everywhere (and went on doing so throughout most of Gloria's career), so when Gloria was asked to understudy Sabina in *The Skin of Our Teeth* at the Plymouth Theatre in New York, Mother went with her. She coached Gloria in the part that turned out to be her first important break, that of the young Scots barmaid in a play called *Highland Fling*, which was directed by George Abbott. From that performance Gloria was asked to play a very good part in the Broadway production of *The World's Full of Girls*. She was spotted by Louis B. Mayer, taken back to California and put under contract to MGM.

Small parts in films like *Blonde Fever*, *Without Love* and

It Happened in Brooklyn followed before Gloria made an impact in the movies. She was hired out by MGM to the RKO Studio to play the coarse and sluttish tart in the controversial film *Crossfire*, directed by Edward Dmytryk. Gloria was nominated for her first Academy Award.

'I wish that Gloria would have tried harder,' Mother said. 'She was just as good an actress as that other blonde girl.'

'Who are you talking about, Mother?' Gloria shouted from the kitchen, agitated by having to listen to her mother's reminiscences.

'Oh you know, dear,' Mother replied. 'That nice girl who had the affair with the President.'

'It's true, Peter.' Joy leant forward and spoke to me confidentially. 'Gloria would never apply herself properly. She'd never talk to the columnists. I used to get them on the phone going crazy. "That girl's going to ruin her career if she won't talk to me," they used to say. But Gloria would never talk. She's always hated gossip; even though she created quite a lot. And she'd never dress herself properly. When we used to go over to Zsa Zsa's house, her mother would say, "Oh that Gloria. She could make something of herself. If she'd only fix herself up a bit." But that's Gloria, Peter. She's impossible. She didn't even wear a new dress when she won an Oscar! She just threw on a mink. Gloria likes to do things her way.'

'That's enough talking about me,' Gloria called out. 'Save your mouths for dinner. It's ready.'

After the meal Mother fell asleep and Joy brought Gloria up to date on family news until it was time for them to leave.

The sun had set. The evening was warm and lovely. Gloria and I sat together by the edge of the pool.

'Why don't you like people talking about your career?' I asked. 'Don't you like being an actress?'

'Yeah, sure I like being an actress. But that's why I like it when we're in England. It means something there. I just don't like this movie-star stuff. It's nothing. Sometimes I wish I'd have continued on the New York stage instead of going to Metro. Maybe that might have worked out well. Who knows?' She shrugged her shoulders and nestled her head against my chest.

'Let's go for a drive along the coast,' I said. 'It's a beautiful night.'

'Oh let's do that, Peter!' Her face lit up. 'It'll be fun. You can practise using the car.'

We stopped off in a parking lot on the way towards Malibu and sat on the bonnet, looking out across the ocean. There were little bonfires burning along the beach where people were having parties and, somewhere, someone was playing a guitar. The sky was a magenta colour and seemed to be lit from behind with golden rays. The moon was full and sat on the surface of the ocean. It was the most stunning evening sky.

'Oh Peter! Look what's happening!' Gloria jumped off the front of the car and ran towards the beach.

I could hear other voices, shouting. There was tremendous excitement.

'Quick, Peter! Quick, come and take a look! The grunion are running! The grunion are running!'

I looked down on the beach. There were thousands of silver-coloured fish twisting and jumping, circling and flapping. The beach was a mass of silver. The little shimmering fish were washed up on the sand by a wave, another would take them back to the sea again. The grunion were on the run. It only happens once in a while.

'Peter . . .'

I dreamt Gloria had called my name. I moved. I was warm until I moved but then I was cold. It was morning. It was light, a running-water coloured light. I could almost feel the rain as it hit the window and imagined how long each drop was taking to slide down the glass.

The couch I was lying on was at an angle and I'd been sleeping in a groove. I was covered by a coat, my horrible old overcoat, and a bit of a blanket. The coat was torn and I was caught up in the lining and, because I'd moved, my back was only covered by a sleeve.

'Peter . . .'

It wasn't a dream. It was Gloria who'd called my name. I threw off the coat and the blanket and ran down the stairs to the middle room.

She was looking towards the door waiting for me to arrive.

'I didn't hear you,' I said. 'I've just woken up. Are you okay?'

'I guess I'm okay.' She turned away. 'I thought you were going to stay in here, Peter. You said that you were going to sleep on that other little bed right there. You sneaked off.'

'You fell asleep and I didn't want to disturb you.'

'Hmm,' she sighed. 'That wouldn't have mattered.'

Gloria was mad at me for leaving her by herself. I recognized the expression. It was just like a New York morning. She would get up early and disappear into the bathroom to take a shower and put on her make-up. Eventually she would return looking glamorous, but pouting and sulking heavily. If I'd fallen asleep again she would wake me up with bits of breakfast, which usually consisted of a glass of milk mixed with lecithin granules and vitamin B powder. Then the pills: a calcium magnesium, a 'C' and a 'D'. After that I'd get a cold boiled egg, a strange piece of toast and an apricot kernel. Coffee would come last. She'd stop sulking when I'd say something nice and then we'd get on with the rest of the day. I always enjoyed her morning sulks.

Even though she was ill and uncomfortable, the sight of her sulking now was pathetic and sweet and it made me sad.

'Your hair looks nice.'

'Your mother fixed it,' she said.

'You look much better today.'

'I feel much better.'

'Do you want me to get you anything?'

'Your mother's done everything for me. She's already been in and helped me out.'

It was obvious that my mother had been about. The covers on the bed looked neat and tidy and there was a cup of tea on the table next to it. Gloria looked fresh and alert and her hair did look presentable. She really was looking better than she had the night before.

'I'm going down to the kitchen,' I said. 'And then I'm going to the health food shop.'

'Okay, Peter, but don't forget the grape juice. I need the black grape juice. And get me that book by Adele Davis, it's called *Let's Get Well*.'

'Do you want me to get you some magazines?'

'No, thanks, Peter. I don't want to look at a magazine.'

'Do you want me to bring you a radio?'

'No, thanks, Peter. I don't want to listen to the radio. I just want to be alone. I'm thinking.'

The window was open. It was cold so I closed it.

'No, don't do that,' she said. 'Please leave it open. I want the window open.'

My mother was on her knees sorting out the cupboards underneath the kitchen sink.

'I was just coming to wake you.' She looked up as I came through the door.

'There's no need for you to be doing that, is there? It's a bit early in the day.'

'If it wasn't for me, nothing would ever get done in this house. Joe's been on the phone –' she stood up to tell me – 'and he wants you to meet him in that health food shop in Lower Breck Road. He hasn't got time to come here and collect you. He's got to do something to the car.'

'What time did he say?'

'Round about eleven, so you'd better get a move on,' she added, looking towards the clock. 'It's just turned half past nine.'

Breakfast of bacon, eggs and toast was instantly produced and my mother got back down to clearing away the pots and pans with a determined look in her eye. We didn't mention Gloria but I wasn't convinced that she was really absorbed in her household chores, so I sat in silence eating the food. When she started to dismantle parts of the gas stove and began cleaning the steel grill with a knife, I thought that perhaps it might be wise to speak.

'I had a terrible sleep,' I said.

'I'm not surprised. I covered you with a blanket. I don't know why you didn't get into bed.'

'I stayed up to telephone Gloria's daughter in California,' I explained. 'I must have fallen asleep.'

'And what did she have to say?' My mother sat down at the table. 'When is she coming here? Did you tell her that we want to take Gloria to the hospital?'

'She wasn't at home,' I said. 'I'll try again later.'

'Well somebody's got to come.' My mother looked alarmed. 'Because if they don't I won't be going to Australia on no holiday. I wouldn't go away and leave somebody sick in my house. I just couldn't do that. I'll have to look after Gloria.'

'Don't worry,' I said. 'I'm going to call the doctor when we get back. We'll try to get Gloria to go to the hospital. Everything will be all right.' I stood up to leave the room. 'Anyway, Mum. Why were you awake in the night?'

'Because I had a terrible sleep as well,' she said. 'And so did Gloria. I heard her call out in the night.'

'Did you open the window in her room?'

'Yes,' my mother replied. 'I had to. The room was beginning to smell.'

Gloria's teenage daughter, Paulette, used the trailer in California as a home base, but she sometimes stayed with friends. I was worried that if she wasn't at home there would be no immediate way that I could contact the rest of the family. I dialled the number again. This time she was there to answer my call.

I explained that Gloria was ill and that she was with me at the house in Liverpool.

'Oh, I know that she's sick, Peter, but I thought that she'd got much better. She took good care of herself while she was here in the trailer. That's why she left for England. She ate fresh vegetables and broth and she got herself much better. She looked really pretty and she was relaxed. She tended the garden and did dishes and things. She was preparing herself to do the play.'

'Well, she's not doing the play any more. She's very seriously ill. The doctor who saw her in Lancaster advised me that she should have an operation, but she won't go back to the hospital. She won't go to any hospital. It's difficult to know what to do.'

'Just feed her with broth, Peter. Mom likes to heal herself. She doesn't trust doctors. She's always healed herself.'

'Yes, I know that, Paulette, but now I'm afraid it's got more complicated. I'd like you to phone her sister, Joy, and ask her to call me here in England. I think that someone should come as soon as possible.'

'Can I speak to Mom, please, Peter?'

'No, you can't. It's impossible for her to get to the telephone. She's too ill. Besides, she's asked me not to worry you.'

'Okay, Peter. I understand. I'll ask Joy to call you and I'll speak with you again later. I'm sure that Mom will get much better. She just needs plenty of rest.'

The health food shop was at the end of a small Victorian terrace, sandwiched between a pet shop, with a window full of sleepy, shiny black Labrador dogs, and a haberdasher, displaying a window full of knitting patterns, needles and wool. It wasn't like the health stores I was used to seeing in almost every London high street; it was more a cross between an old-fashioned chemist and a second-hand bookshop. There were no delicious smells coming from freshly cooked vegetable lasagnes and newly baked banana and date cakes; there were no tubs of brown rice, lentils and muesli. But there was a postcard in the window saying 'Vegan needs own space in mixed house. Non-smoker. No hang-ups'. It seemed curiously out of place.

Except for one wall which was completely covered by books, the shop was furnished with clumsy old mahogany and plate-glass display cases. There was a glass bell-shaped jar on the counter half full of barley sugar lollipops and the shelves were lined with bottles of vitamin pills, homeopathic and Bach flower remedies.

The woman behind the counter was standing on a ladder and holding a heavy-looking black leather-bound account book from which she was checking items off against a list. She looked as if she'd always been old. Her tinted hair was falling out of its perm, her shoes were plain and sensible and the white doctor's coat she was wearing fell well below her knees. She'd stuffed a thick woollen sweater that had a roll collar underneath the white coat which made her head look smaller than it should be and her chest much bigger than it could have been. Everything about her was out of proportion. She looked slightly deformed.

'Hello,' I said and moved up close to the counter.

The woman didn't reply but turned towards a closed door that led to the back of the shop. It opened and out came a man, also wearing a white coat, who was about the same age as the woman. He looked at me suspiciously, as if he was signalling to somebody else behind my back, but I was the only customer.

'I'm just looking around,' I said.

The man carried on staring at me as if there was something very wrong. I quickly checked my person for defects. Had I forgotten to put socks on, things like that? Everything seemed to be in order except that I was wearing my horrible old overcoat, and I hadn't had time to shave and, because it was raining hard, my hair was stuck to my face. I must have looked a mess. The man looked at the woman, the woman looked at me and then they looked at each other. I edged to the back of the shop and began to go through the books, hoping that Joe and Jessie would arrive soon.

Besides *Let's Get Well*, which Gloria had specifically asked me to get her, I found lots of other books about illness, its prevention and cure. I turned to the sections on cancer and studied each one carefully.

There were many varying opinions but most of the writers agreed that cancer was a disease characterized by body cell growth gone completely haywire. One author thought it was a social problem, not a medical one. His opinion was that the health of the nation was in the hands of the food industrialists who made big money out of food production and distribution. The government was responsible for causing cancer, he thought, by allowing the food industrialists to spray crops and vegetables with chemicals, rather than making them fertilize the soil naturally. It was also up to the government, he said, to encourage people to alter their attitudes towards food and diet. The man's argument made absolute sense to me but I wasn't comforted by his words of wisdom. I didn't have the time to lobby politicians. I wanted a solution now.

In his book *Victory Over Cancer*, Mr Cyril Scott came to the conclusion that one of the primary causes of cancer is a deficiency of potassium in the blood and he advised taking a teaspoon of crude molasses every day to help towards prevention. Again, his words were convincing and his argument very plausible, but Gloria already had cancer. I wanted to find a miracle cure.

Mr Scott went on to say that he thought orthodox treatment of burning cancer growths away with rays or cutting them with a knife wouldn't achieve a thing because another growth could easily form. It occurred to me that maybe Gloria had read this book and that was why she was determined not to have an operation, why she didn't want to go back to hospital, because she didn't want to be cut up. 'Mom likes to heal herself,' that's what Paulette had said to me on the telephone, so I must make it possible for her to do that. I must help Gloria to find a natural health cure.

I took down from the shelf Dr Kirstin Nolfi's book *The Raw Food Treatment of Cancer and Other Diseases*. This lady cured herself of cancer by fasting on vegetable juices for thirty to forty days.

'I'll follow this advice,' I thought. 'I'll supervise Gloria on a fast.' Then I realized that I didn't have forty days to spare. I had to get my mother to Australia by the middle of the next week. In the meantime she would think that I was trying to murder Gloria rather than helping her to get well if I put her on a lunatic fast for a month.

I was confused and distraught as I read up on other suggestions for curing this horrible disease. Then I found Mr Frank Wilson's book *Food For The Golden Age*.

'The capacity of the body for healthfulness is truly immense,' he wrote. 'There is always the chance of letting nature have a go though one cannot expect miracles.' He went on to say, 'If a disease like cancer is diagnosed, have it operated on and removed if it is not too late . . . to rely on nature to cure in a monstrously unnatural situation is to court certain death in many cases. With nature cures, cancers do heal – at times – but one would have a much better chance if one had the cancer removed and then followed it up on the road to health with nature.'

I felt depressed. I wanted to help her but I didn't know how.

'Just what can I ever do to make her get better?' I said to myself and put my hands to my head. 'What can I do about my mother getting to Australia? I don't want to spoil her holiday. Where's Joe? Where's Jessie? I need Joe and Jessie.'

The tiredness and the hysteria of the last twenty-four hours had caught up on me. I realized that I was slumped with my head against the bookshelves talking to myself out loud. I was gabbling. The people behind the counter must have thought that I was cracked. I was certainly behaving as if I was. These books were not going to help me to help Gloria.

'What are you doing in here?' The voice sounded hard and aggressive.

I turned towards the counter. It was the man in the white coat. Both he and the woman were looking at me as if I were a dangerous madman. I was overcome with embarrassment and felt the redness rise in my cheeks.

'What are you doing in here?' the man repeated.

'I'm looking for a cure for cancer,' I replied.

'Well you can look elsewhere,' the man barked.

'But I want to buy some apricot kernels and I'm supposed to meet my brother here at eleven o'clock.'

'We don't have any apricot kernels and you can wait for your brother outside.' He pointed to the door. 'This is not a waiting room, it's a shop.'

'I can't do that,' I said. 'It's raining.'

'Right!' The woman turned to the man. 'Let's call the police.'

'That's a bit ridiculous,' I protested. 'A friend of mine is very ill. I've come here to try and help her. I'm just waiting for my brother, and I have to buy some grape juice.'

'Buy your grape juice somewhere else. Just get out of this shop!'

'I'm trying to help someone who is very sick with cancer,' I emphasized. 'That's why I'm looking through your books. Don't you understand?'

'Get out!' the man shouted. 'Clear off out of my shop!'

Suddenly I was in a fury.

'You shouldn't be allowed to run a health food shop. You're not concerned about anybody's health. You should be struck off a list!' I raged. 'This is not a healthy shop. It's an unhealthy fucking shop!'

I was in the middle of a slanging match, assaulting the

man with every insult and foul word that I could think of, when Joe and Jessie arrived. I'd made myself so angry that tears were rolling down my face. The incident had let loose all the emotion I'd been holding in. The couple behind the counter huddled themselves together as Joe dragged me screaming from the shop.

Outside on the pavement my brother was laughing so much that he was making the same groaning and whining noises that I was. Then the Labrador dogs in the window of the pet shop next door started to do the same. Joe, Jessie and myself ended up standing in a fit of uncontrollable, helpless laughter in the rain. The two white coats were looking at us through the glass panel in their shop door. They were horrified. Jessie realized that we might not be able to buy the things we needed anywhere else, so she went back to try and make peace with the man and the woman, but as she approached the door they bolted it and pulled down the blind.

We went to do the shopping somewhere else.

The kitchen was empty when we arrived back home with the shopping; not even Candy was there, lying as she normally did in front of the gas fire. But there was a note from my mother: 'Gone to Tesco's' it read.

The day was brighter. It had stopped raining. A stream of sunlight projected across the room, holding in suspension a constellation of dancing dust. An unexpected calm filled the room.

'There's no need to worry about that tree.' Joe stood by the window looking out. 'I think it's going to be all right.'

'Oh, I hope it is. I've always liked that tree, I don't want it to fall down,' Jessie said as she put on the kettle.

For a few moments it seemed just like any other afternoon.

Then in an instant we realized, it was as if we'd almost forgotten: Gloria was in the middle room. There was no one else in the house. She was alone.

There was no need for panic.

'I've been trying to make a plait.' Gloria was sitting up in the bed trying to twist strands of her hair together with one hand and holding the piece of broken mirror with the other. 'Didn't you see *"10"*, the movie?' She gave me a quizzical look.

Gloria was animated and chatty, creating a party-like atmosphere in the room. As she laughed we relaxed.

'You two men can leave us alone now,' Jessie said. 'I've bought Gloria a nice nightdress to wear and she wants to put it on, don't you, Gloria?'

'I sure do,' she replied.

As we closed the door to the bedroom we heard Jessie and Gloria laugh.

'She's going to pull through,' Joe said as we went down to the kitchen. 'I've got a very strong feeling that she is definitely going to pull through.'

He searched round the kitchen for something to eat, opened the fridge and found a kipper.

'Just what I fancy,' he said and tossed the kipper into the frying pan.

While it sizzled away, its delicious smell wafting around the room, I sat in the armchair in the corner, hoping, like Joe, that everything was going to be all right. Maybe the worst was over, maybe the tables had turned. Even the tree in the garden looked friendly for once, instead of alarming. Then Jessie burst into the room.

'Gloria wants a kipper. She can smell it in her room. It's coming up through the floor. It's the first thing she's wanted to eat. Maybe she's getting better. Oh Peter, isn't it wonderful! Gloria wants to eat a kipper!'

We were excited, ecstatic, high on kippers, and ran round the kitchen bumping into each other in a race to find a knife and fork, some bread, butter for the bread and a tray to arrange everything on. Joe folded two squares of kitchen roll to make them look like a napkin and Jessie ceremoniously carried the tray holding the kipper, the amazing kipper, the life-saving kipper, up to the middle room. Joe and I followed behind in attendance.

Gloria, looking sweet in her new nightgown and her attempted Bo Derek hairstyle, squealed with delight when we brought the kipper into the room. Joe and Jessie sat at the end of the bed. I sat at the side and we waited for her to take the first bite.

It was awful; it was obvious that she couldn't do it. Gloria tried to swallow but she just couldn't eat. She pretended that it didn't matter, and yet it must have been agony for her.

The house was gloomy again.

My mother was in the kitchen. She had quietly returned from Tesco's and was putting the shopping into the cupboards. She didn't say anything, only glanced at the kipper as it was carried over to the sink. She was still wearing her coat but her headscarf had fallen about her shoulders as if she didn't care, as if she was in a daze.

'I've bought some boiled ham for a sandwich. It's there if anybody wants it.'

'I don't fancy anything,' Jessie said. Then holding the kipper up on the plate she added, 'We cooked this for Gloria but she couldn't eat it.'

'Oh,' my mother said. 'Oh, poor Gloria. And the smell of kippers lasts for ages.'

'What's wrong with you, Mam, you look a bit fed up? The kettle's been on, I'll make a pot of tea.'

'I'm all right, Joe,' my mother replied. Then she sat down at the table and dropped her head into her hands. It wasn't her usual dramatic gesture but much more subdued. 'A doctor's been on the phone from Lancaster.' She looked up at me. 'He wants you to call him back. He's left a number.'

'What did he want?' I asked.

'He wanted to tell us,' she said, 'that Gloria's got forty-eight hours to live.'

Then she started to cry.

'Oooh,' the woman said. 'I'm afraid that you're stuck.'

'Well how do I get unstuck?' I asked. 'You're the area health authority. The doctor from Lancaster advised me to telephone you. He told me you'd be able to help.'

'Mmm,' she said. 'Not really. No, I don't think I can. From what you've just explained it seems to me like a catch 22 situation.'

'I don't understand.'

'You'll have to speak up, dear. I've got a crackle on my line.'

47

'I don't understand,' I repeated. 'I don't know what you mean.'

'Well,' she said, 'let me put it this way. If your friend is refusing to go to a hospital and you, or anyone else, try to take her to one against her wishes, then you, or whoever it is, could be charged with an assault. It's a criminal offence. Also, let's say for instance that if she happened to have a heart attack, or catch pneumonia, or died of fright, or anything unfortunate happened to her on the way to the hospital, well, love, you could easily find yourself up for a manslaughter.'

'Oh no,' I said.

'Oh yes,' she asserted. 'It's a very tricky one because on the one hand if you don't get anyone to take a look at your friend, if you don't have any medical help at all, well . . .' She paused and tut-tut-tutted. 'I hate to think but I imagine that there would be a hell of an inquest.'

'Why?' I asked. 'Why a hell of an inquest?'

'Well,' she explained. 'If she does die, and you say that a doctor seems to think that she will, then you're going to have a problem phoning the police and explaining to them that you've got a dead American actress up in your back bedroom, aren't you, son? It is a bit unusual.'

'Yes, but how can you help me? You've got to help me. I don't know what to do.'

'You've got a young voice,' the woman said. 'How old are you?'

'Twenty-nine,' I answered.

'Mm . . .' she paused, 'I've got a thought . . .'

The idea was that as Gloria was a guest at the house she

48

couldn't really object to another guest being invited, who happened to be a doctor.

Doctor Casey, a small, elderly man who spoke with a gentle Irish accent, arrived a few hours later. He was semi-retired, had a private practice and lived locally.

My mother opened the door to the doctor and showed him into the living room, the room reserved for strangers or important people. With the exception of my father, who was still out with the dog, we were all standing uneasily waiting for him to arrive. I was by the window under the hanging plants. Joe and Jessie stood by the sideboard with the glass doors, behind which were displayed a hoard of ornaments which my mother had been given over the years by other members of the family who'd been on holidays to Wales or Blackpool or the Isle of Man. At each end of the sideboard stood two chalk black cats which promised good luck from Ireland and between them, on one leg, stood a Flamenco dancer in a black twirling frock, which my sister Maisie brought back from Benidorm.

My mother had given instructions to the effect that, as she was now taking control of the situation, we had to keep our mouths shut in front of the doctor until she had had her say. He, however, spoke first.

'There's an awful lot of photographs that you have around the room,' he said.

'Yes, Doctor,' my mother replied. 'They're just some pictures of my family.'

'It's an awful lot of family that you have,' he looked concerned.

'Yes, Doctor. I've got five sons, four daughters, thirty-four grandchildren and twenty-seven great-grandchildren, I married very young.'

'Phew! Mother of God! You must be a very strong and healthy woman.'

'Oh I am, Doctor,' my mother agreed. 'But I do have a permanent backache and I've had chronic bronchitis since the war.'

'Oh that's a terrible complaint. Does it affect your nerves?'

'Oh yes, Doctor. Me nerves have been badly affected, but not so much as they are now with all this going on in the house.'

'Yes,' he sympathized. 'It's a terrible situation that you have on your hands. Everything has been explained to me by the health authorities.'

'And I've got to get to Australia next week!' she declared. 'I've got a passage booked on the aeroplane. I couldn't go and leave this girl the way she is, doctor, but I've got to go and see my son who I haven't seen for sixteen years. Gloria should be in a hospital. She should be having proper medical attention and care.'

'Shall I go and tell Gloria that you're here, Doctor?' I could see that my mother was getting a bit too worked up.

'Oh no,' he replied. 'Let's not get her into a panic with a warning. I'll just go up to the room and you can introduce me. Don't worry, I'll be very gentle.'

As I opened the living room door we caught sight of my father hurrying into the kitchen. Candy followed behind.

'Hello there,' he said, red in the face. He'd been caught off guard listening at the door.

'And how are you?' asked Doctor Casey.

'Smashing,' my father replied. 'Bloody smashing.'

Gloria was looking desolate. Her Bo Derek plait had completely fallen out and was hanging limp down the side of her face. She was thinking, staring vacantly, just thinking.

'Gloria.' I knelt by the side of the bed. 'There's a man here to see you. He's a doctor.'

'Oh no, Peter,' she cried.

I left them alone in the room. I felt as if I had betrayed her.

'You're just out to embarrass me.'

I could hear my mother's voice coming from the kitchen as I waited in the hall to speak to Doctor Casey.

'I don't know what that doctor will think of you,' she said. 'Listening from behind the door. You're a grown man, not a big, soft kid.'

'No one tells me what goes on in this house,' I heard my father reply.

'Ah,' the doctor said, joining me at the foot of the stairs. 'It's always a pitiful sight. I'm afraid to have to tell you that I agree with what you've already been told. I don't think that your friend is going to be with us for very long.'

I sat down on the stairs.

'Well,' he continued. 'She's beginning to lose her body fluids and I wouldn't be surprised if she slips into a coma.'

'What will happen if she does?'

'Oh, at first she'll go into a very deep sleep and then you'll let me know.'

'Does she know what's happening?'

'I should think that she might have an idea. She's confused but she's putting up a fight. Although an operation would now be pointless, I tried to persuade her into going to a hospital, but as we know, she's having none of that.'

'Is she in any pain?' I asked.

'No,' Doctor Casey replied. 'At the moment I don't think that she is.'

The last thing that I wanted to do was to leave the house and even less appear in a play.

'In a bit of a rush again tonight, are we?' Old Jack peered at me through the open door of his office.

'Yes, I'm sorry I'm late,' I said. 'I've got a bit of a problem.'

'Like to tell Uncle Jack all about it?'

'No, thanks,' I replied. 'It's a bit personal.'

'I'm always interested to know what's happening,' he said and gave a filthy grin.

'Look,' I said, 'just piss off. Someone's dying.'

'Oooh, anyone I know?'

'I shouldn't think you do. She's American. She's a film star.'

'Let's not be silly,' he said. 'Film stars don't die in Liverpool.'

The character I was playing had thirty-six stage entrances in the first act of the play, almost as many in the second, and it seemed as though I mistimed every one of them. I was tired, my body was functioning on remote control and my concentration was elsewhere. At one point I spoke some of my lines before Geoffrey had finished speaking his, causing a tricky situation on the stage and an outburst in the Green Room after the performance.

I couldn't be bothered. I just left the theatre as hastily as I could.

'Good,' I thought, when I heard the stage door bang shut behind me. 'I've got that over with until tomorrow and it's not raining. Thank God it's not raining. I'll walk some of the way home.'

Before I reached the corner of the street I heard the stage door bang shut again and someone came running after me.

'Hold on, Pete. Wait for me.'

Gil was fastening up her coat and putting on a hat.

'You're in a rush,' she said when she caught up with me. 'You're like a bloody locomotive. I tried to speak to you last night and tonight, but you disappeared before I could open my mouth.'

'Oh I'm sorry, everything's been going wrong. I messed things up a bit.'

'Everybody does sometime. It's happened to us all. Don't worry about it.'

'Thanks,' I said and we walked on in silence.

'I heard that bust up between you and Geoffrey,' she said after a while. 'Don't worry about it. He's under a lot of strain. We all are.'

'Has he got another job to go to after this?'

'Maybe he hasn't.'

'I hope something turns up,' I said.

Problems like that were something other people could identify with, something which was easily understood. Perhaps mine was too removed from reality to be taken seriously. 'Film stars don't die in Liverpool,' Old Jack had said. 'That's right,' I thought. 'It just doesn't seem real.'

All the lights were on, all the doors were open; I arrived home in the middle of a panic. Candy, flapping and whimpering, was waiting for me in the hall and my father, dressed in his pyjamas, was standing outside his bedroom door.

'Quick! You're wanted on the phone,' he said. 'Joe's talking on it now. It's just rung two minutes ago. Quick! It's someone from America.'

'Paulette tells me that her mother is not feeling so good. Is that right, Peter?'

'Yes, Joy. Gloria is very sick.'

'Is she eating properly, Peter?'

'Now look, Joy. You must listen very carefully. Your sister can't eat. She is desperately ill. She has cancer in her stomach. She's dying. She's about to go into a coma.'

'I had no idea, Peter. I'm absolutely stunned. I knew that she had been ill, that's why she came out to the coast. I didn't like the idea of her going to England to do the play but she was determined. She said that she was better. You know how she is, Peter. You know Gloria.'

'Joy, will you come to Liverpool? It's important that someone comes over here immediately.'

'Of course. I'll try, Peter. Someone will definitely come. I'll see what I can arrange and call you back in your morning. I'll find out what can be done and I'll call you back. I'll hang up now. I'm upset.'

'Is she on her way then?' my father enquired as I passed through the hall. He was standing as before with Candy by his side.

'Yes,' I said. 'She's making the arrangements.'

'That's bloody marvellous. Did you hear that, Bella?' He opened the door wider and shouted into the room. 'Peter says she's on her way.'

'Thank Christ for that,' was my mother's reply.

He disappeared behind the door and the light in their bedroom was switched out.

Candy followed me into the kitchen.

'Is she really on her way?' Joe asked, handing me a mug of hot tea. 'She didn't seem too sure to me.'

'She's making the arrangements,' I told him. 'She's going to see what she can do.'

'Now that's not good enough, Peter. It's just not good enough. Somebody has definitely got to get over here because time's running out and a lot of decisions will have to be made. Gloria should be in a nursing home. We all know that, and yet we can't take her anywhere unless she herself decides to go. You'll have to persuade her, Peter. You'll have to go up to her room and talk her round. It will be the best thing for Gloria, and for you, and for me mam and everybody. Gloria is dying. The woman is dying. Do you understand? She's about to go into a coma.'

'Yes,' I said. 'I understand.'

Everything Joe said made sense but I just felt completely numb. I couldn't be practical. I couldn't change the situation. I just wanted it to go away. Gloria was dying; I didn't want her to, but there was nothing I could do.

'She's getting worse, Peter,' Jessie said when she joined us in the kitchen. 'Ever since the doctor was here she's deteriorated. I think that she knows. She's gone very quiet. She's hardly spoke. She just looks at you, waits and wants to be burped. I think she's frightened.'

'Have you been with her all evening?' I asked.

'A lot of the time,' Jessie answered. 'We all have. She can't be left alone. She's got to have someone with her every minute. Just in case, well, you know, just in case.'

'I'll go up to her now,' I said. 'I'll stay with her the night.'

'No, you don't have to do that,' Joe said. 'Me and Jessie are staying tonight to help out.'

'Yes, we've worked it all out, Peter. We're to spend turns apiece. If you go now, I'll take over from you, Joe will take over from me and your mother will go in to her in the morning. That way she won't be left alone and we'll all get a bit of sleep.'

Gloria looked impassive and remote. Her hair had been brushed out of its plaits, accidentally leaving a flick and a wave over one eye, a style I'd often seen her try to create. She closed her eyes and turned her head towards the wall, then sighed. 'The light,' she said. 'It's bright.'

I put the lamp on the floor and covered the top of the shade so that the light was only dim.

'I'll go out and buy a pink bulb tomorrow,' I thought. I knew that's what she'd like.

I moved away to sit on the other bed.

It was strange and yet familiar to be lying together in a darkened room, silent, both thinking. When I got cold I pulled the blanket up around me and put my head against the pillows. It was an uneasy comfort that I felt.

'Do you want anything?' I asked.

'Yes,' she replied. 'The light. I want you to put it out.'

For a while we were in total blackness but when the curtains were lit up by the moon passing from behind a cloud, my eyes got used to the dark and I could see her clearly. Her eyes were open. She was concentrating hard. She looked determined.

The shape of the window was reflected on the door but at an angle which made it look bigger. Nothing was in perspective. The branches of the tree that leant towards the house made shadows on the walls and on the ceiling. When I traced each shadow carefully I saw pictures in the shapes. It must have been a picture that led me into a dream.

The singing woke me up; the sound of a girl's voice, sweet and appealing, was coming from the room above.

Poor wand'ring one! Tho' thou hast surely strayed,
Take heart of grace. Thy steps retrace. Poor wand'ring one!
Poor wand'ring one! If such poor love as mine
Can help thee find. True peace of mind. Why take it,
It is thine.

'Peter,' Gloria's voice suddenly punctuated the melody. 'You kissed me when you had a cold.'

Startled by the sound of Gloria's voice, my breath disappeared. I was left searching for words while the singing went on, louder, harder, the voice getting stronger, now joined by another. I couldn't speak.

Take heart, no danger lowers; Take any heart but ours!
Take heart, fair days will shine; Take any heart, take mine!
Take heart, no danger lowers; Take any heart but ours!
Take heart, fair days will shine; Take any heart, take mine!
Ah–h–h!

A voice soared into a cadenza.

'It's ruined my stomach, Peter,' Gloria added.

An aria accompanied my thoughts; my mind went into a spin, until I realized what she was talking about: almost two years earlier, when she was appearing in a play in London, I'd had a cold, so she took a whole tube of vitamin C tablets, the kind that fizz up in water, because she was worried about catching the cold and losing her voice. She never developed the symptoms but she did feel sick the following day.

I turned the light back on and returned the lamp to the table. The room was bright again. The shadows disappeared. The singing suddenly stopped.

'Gloria, if you think that your stomach is ruined, it would be sensible if you went somewhere to make it better again. Please let me take you to a hospital, I'll stay there with you if you want.'

'Do you think I'm fighting for my life, Peter?'

'Yes,' I answered. 'I do.'

'Is that why you called in the doctor, Peter?'

'Yes,' I replied. 'Of course it was. You won't get better if you won't let anyone help you to get better. You need to be looked after properly by someone who knows what they're doing. You see, Gloria, I just don't know what to do.'

'You're doing fine, honey,' she said.

I sat thinking, alone in the upstairs flat. I thought about Gloria taking the vitamin C and remembered her being sick the next day. She was only sick for a day! Vitamin C couldn't cause cancer, could it? I couldn't be to blame, could I? All because I kissed her when I had a cold.

THREE

'Enjoy your stay in England,' Mr Longdon said and smiled so wide that his lips almost touched his ears. He gave Gloria a cautious little squeeze on the elbow and quietly mouthed the words, 'Thank you for banking with us.'

'I'll be back soon.' Delighted, Gloria patted him on the jacket and gave him a winning smile.

That morning she'd been broke, waiting for money to come from America, and now she'd been issued with a cheque book, a cash card, an overdraft facility and a handful of twenty-pound notes.

I'd suggested she go to the bank in Camden Town because it was near to where we were living and also because I'd had dealings with the manager, Mr Longdon, who'd been hand-ling my account for the past few years. He was known to be kind to actors so I was sure he'd be generous and impressed if I took in a film star. He'd be certain to give Gloria an over-draft and maybe, I thought, I might get one too. However, he looked at me and frowned when I joined them at the door to his office.

'And what can I do for you?' he asked.

'Oh, we're together,' Gloria announced.

'But how did you get to know him?'

'Oooh,' she replied. 'I guess I just struck lucky.'

Mr Longdon looked shaken, as if he'd been robbed, when we waved him goodbye and walked out into Camden High Street to catch the bus back up to Adelaide Road.

Although we were living at the same address near Regent's Park, it wasn't until a few weeks after she'd arrived from America that we first met. I was living in a small room at the top of a large Edwardian house and Gloria, while she was over in England working on a play, was renting the spacious ground-floor apartment.

Each morning as I passed through the hallway I would hear noises, movements and strange sounds coming from behind the door.

'Loo Poo Boo Moo.'

'Lah Pah Bah Mah.'

Sometimes I would hear her reciting a rhyme:

'No, said she. Away, said she. A-sitting very prettily by a chestnut tree.'

I was intrigued, curious to meet her. I vaguely knew her name but had no idea who she really was. I had to ask the landlady.

'Of course you know who she is, dahling,' she said, and poured herself a gin. 'Everybody's heard of Gloria Grahame. She's been in every Hollywood film. She had hot coffee thrown in her face! She always played a tart.'

'Oh yes,' I said. 'I think I know who you mean.'

One morning Gloria opened her door and found me hovering in the hall.

'Oh, hi. Have you seen *Saturday Night Fever*?'

'Yes,' I replied.

'Did you like it?'

'Er, yes,' I answered.

'Oh that's good. In that case you can come in and hustle. I have to take a dance class.'

She taught me her routine and we danced in time to the music of 'Stayin' Alive'.

Her movements were rhythmic and slick. Her voice distinctive, lending every word a seductive, breathy lisp. Her face was instantly familiar. I remembered her from *Oklahoma!* as the funny girl who couldn't say no, and as the soft-hearted bitch, the one who didn't get the man, in *The Greatest Show on Earth*, and yes, it was Lee Marvin who threw boiling coffee in her face because she sided up with Glenn Ford in *The Big Heat*. She wasn't wearing fancy clothes, just her usual T-shirt and a pair of jeans. She wore no make-up, only lipstick, which she used to build up the outline of her upper lip, and her hair was a terrible mess. But she looked sensational. Dark glasses and stilettos added an extra touch of glamour. I was captivated. Dazzled by her style.

When the music had finished and the dancing had stopped, exhausted, I realized I ought to go.

'I'll have to leave now,' I said. 'I'm on my way to work.'

'Maybe I'll catch you later.' She clicked her tongue against the roof of her mouth and threw her hair back, then to one side.

'That's probable,' I said. 'I live at the top of the house.'

It was spring. A very hot day in May. The day before had been cloudy and cold, and the sunshine was unexpected. Walking along Regent's Park Road I could see that the local shopkeepers had been affected by the change in the weather. The greengrocer had pulled down his awning so that his produce was protected from the sun, while the ironmonger had folded his up and was busy cleaning the window. Two tables with cloths on sat on the pavement outside the French restaurant at the corner of the street.

'This is great,' I thought as I climbed up the steep path that goes over Primrose Hill. 'Maybe the summer has come.'

I didn't want to make a noise and disturb Gloria when I got home late that night, so I tiptoed past her door on the way to my room. Just as I passed the point on the stairs where they squeak, and then twist round on up to the next floor, I noticed that the door to her rooms was now slightly ajar.

'Is that you upstairs?' she called from behind the door.

'Yes, it's me. It's Peter.'

'Oh Peter,' she said in that devastating voice. 'Peter. So that's who you are. Hmm, I was gonna yell. You might have been a cat burglar or something. This house gives me the creeps.'

'Well, it's only me,' I reassured her. 'It's all right. I think you'll be safe.'

'Oh,' she miaowed, sounding disappointed. 'I just love to be safe.'

Then she closed the door, so I went on up to my room.

A few days later on my way out of the house I'd just passed the squeak on the stairs when I heard the most terrible scream. It was Gloria. I rushed to her room, knocked very loud but there was no answer, so I turned the handle and pushed open the door. Before I could speak she flung herself at it from the other side. It slammed shut and I was pushed against the banister by the impact.

63

'Oh no you don't!' she hollered. 'You can't come in here, whoever you are. I'm dyeing my eyelashes.'

'Oh, I'm sorry,' I said. 'I heard you scream. I thought you'd had an accident.'

'I sure have,' she answered. 'I've spilt the damn stuff. It's gone all over my shirt.'

I was about to leave her to it when her door opened slightly and she spoke to me from behind.

'Hey, Peter,' she whispered. 'You couldn't help me out, could you? I have to get to a rehearsal but now I don't have a shirt. My other one's in the laundry.'

I found her one of my own and left it on the handle of her door.

That night when I returned there was a note waiting for me at the bottom of my bed.

> *Why don't U come down? Let's have a drink.*
> *Gloria.*

So I went.

'Scotch?'

'Yes, okay. Scotch.'

She waltzed over to the cabinet and poured me a huge drink.

Her rooms were bigger than I'd thought they would be. A bathroom and kitchen leading off the sitting room were added extensions to the house. Everything was open plan, with the dining room in the middle of the space, and her bedroom in a recess at the front. The furniture, mostly Habitat standards mixed with a few antiques, was tastefully distributed around the rooms. Had she not taken the bulbs out of the lamps and replaced them all with pink ones, the lighting would have been just right.

'I'm really sorry about this morning. Did I give you a start? I'm sure not gonna play about with that eye-dye stuff any more. I'll have to find a beauty room.'

Her head was wrapped up in a scarf, tied in a knot at the side, the ends of which, like ribbons, hung down over her shoulder. She'd taken off the dark glasses and for the first time I could see her grey-green eyes. Her make-up was immaculate.

'Hey, thanks a lot for the shirt,' she said, tucking it in at the waist. 'I love to wear men's clothes.'

It did look very good on her, I thought, but I knew I'd never get it back.

'Here. Try that.' She handed me the drink and sat down next to me on the couch. Her movie-tone smile failed to put me at my ease. 'I hear you're an actor,' she inquired, and waited for a response.

'That's right,' I replied and swallowed half my drink.

'Do you like political plays?'

'It depends on what they are.'

'Well, you're gonna love *Julius Caesar*. It's very political. "Lend me your ears",' she proclaimed. 'Oooh, that William Shakespeare. My mother's read me every word.'

'I once played Romeo,' I told her, thinking she'd find that interesting.

'Oh my God,' she enthused and gave me a smouldering look. 'Hey, can I ask you something? Are you Welsh?'

Just the way she phrased her words and the incredulous look on her face made me laugh out loud.

'Oh no,' she cried. 'Have I said something dumb?'

'I come from the north. I come from Liverpool.'

'That's really something. I'd really like to go there.'

'Well maybe you will.'

'I don't expect so,' she sighed. 'I'm just here long enough to do my play – I'm Sadie Thompson in *Rain*. Then I'm back to the States.'

'What made you decide to do a play in England?' I asked.

'Because I was invited to. Anyway, it's like coming back to my roots. My father was English and my mother came from Scotland. She was an actress here before she went to America, so I guess it's always been an ambition of mine to work in the English theatre. I was brought up on stories about it.'

'Well, I'm surprised you haven't done it before.'

'I would have loved to, Peter, but I've never had the chance before. I'm not known for working in the theatre, so I suppose people forget to ask. It's the same in America. Occasionally I get to do summer stock but nothing that I really want to do. Last year I played Gillian in *Bell, Book and Candle* at the Spring Lake Summer Theater. Huh! Forget it. I'd like to start my career again,' she declared, 'and only work in the theatre. I don't think I've done enough. Just films.'

'And musicals,' I said, thinking of her singing 'I'm just a girl who can't say no.'

'Oh, I couldn't do a show, Peter. Oh no,' she cried and put her hand up to hide her face. 'I can't sing. I couldn't carry a song, not even in a bucket. When I did *Oklahoma!* we had to go through my numbers note by every little note. I warned Dick Rodgers about giving me the part but he just said he was after the twinkle in my eye. Huh, I guess that's all he got.' She bit on her lower lip and started to giggle.

For someone who had been in over thirty Hollywood films alongside great actors like Joan Crawford and Humphrey Bogart, and worked with brilliant directors like Fritz Lang and Vincent Minnelli, Gloria gave me the impression that she had no real sense of achievement.

'It's not the work that I've done that matters so much,' she said. 'It's the work that I want to do that's really important to me. When I get back to New York I wanna work as much as I can in the theatre. I'm gonna go to lots of auditions.'

Her girlish charm and enthusiasm I found irresistible and, within an hour or so, we had become friends. We talked a lot about the things we'd done and she told me lots about working in Hollywood. Most of all she made me laugh.

'Hey, Peter,' she said when I stood up to go. 'Did you go to RADA?'

'No,' I replied. 'I didn't.'

'Well, my mother did! Isn't that something? She taught me everything I know. You must have heard me doing my voice exercises in the morning?'

'Yes, I hear you quite a lot.'

I wished her goodnight and went up to my room. As I reached the top of the stairs I could hear her down below.

'Loo Poo Boo Moo.'

'Lah Pah Bah Mah.'

Rain opened and was moderately successful, although some people thought that Gloria was miscast in the role of Sadie Thompson. She'd been nervous and unsure throughout the rehearsal period, mainly because of her lack of experience of performing in the theatre, and this was apparent on the first night. However, she gained strength through performance and the production was enthusiastically received by each audience.

Although she intended her British debut to be a quiet affair, it was obvious that most of the audience came to the little theatre at Watford, outside London, just to see her. She was inundated with fan mail and her telephone rang constantly. Reporters wanted interviews and photographers started turning up at the house. The interest shown by the press was surprising. There was a double page spread of photographs of her in one of the Sunday magazines, and a national newspaper ran an article calling her a 'legendary floozie'. Invitations to cocktail parties, film premieres and first nights at West End theatres arrived in her post. It was as if she had been rediscovered and was now a celebrity around town. When I escorted her to a party after the opening of a film, she was mobbed by photographers flashing cameras as soon as she stepped out of the taxi.

More important to her than being feted by the glitterati and press, she was immediately asked to appear in *A Tribute to Lili Lamont* at the New End Theatre in London, and was offered a part in a television play with Jim Dale and another with Joseph Cotton. The attention she was getting in England obviously reverberated across the Atlantic: she was approached about appearing in a well-known soap opera and was offered an exciting cameo role in a film called *Head Over Heels*.

Gloria was amused by the roles being offered to her, which ranged from glamorous mistresses to fairy-tale wicked witches and quirky, sexy mothers-in-law.

Gloria and I had now known each other for about three months. We started spending more and more time together, either having meals in her rooms or taking late night walks through London. Mostly we'd end up by the Thames and would walk along the Embankment. She loved to hear me talk about Liverpool. She was fascinated by the place and determined to visit it as soon as she could. Liverpool, to Gloria, held the same fascination as Hollywood did for me. While I'd be wanting her to tell me stories about the movies, she'd be wanting me to tell her stories about my family;

'When did your sister Bella marry Jimmy?'

'Bella married Arthur. It was Mary who married Jimmy.'

'I thought Maisie got him.'

'She did, but that was a different Jimmy.'

'Tell me again how John met Rose?'

'He was staying the weekend with Joe and Jessie and she was the girl next door.'

'. . . and they've been married ever since?'

'Yes, they've got six kids.'

'They must all be so in love. Liverpool sounds heaven.'

When I told her that my sister Eileen was married to an Arab and now lived in Baghdad, she nearly fainted on the spot.

'Oh, that's the most romantic thing I've ever heard.'

I wasn't sure if Eileen would quite agree.

'. . . and tell me more about *you*. I wanna hear all about Betty.'

'I was only five or six,' I pleaded. 'Betty was just a kid from across the street.'

'Well why did you call her Boo Boo?'

The questions went on and on. Gloria was obsessed. She loved me to tell her stories; about my mother in the war, about my father making toys out of old bits of wood to give to us all at Christmas. She could make me recount to her adventures of childhood summer holidays spent on the beach at New Brighton, of the fun whole families had following Bessie Braddock around the streets of Toxteth in the late fifties, carrying 'Vote Labour' placards. Gloria loathed right wing politics and politicians.

'I can't stand the sight of Ronnie Reagan,' she said. 'I'd like to stick my Oscar up his arse!'

One day she received an invitation to visit a London film school to sit through a screening of one of her films.

'Why don't you come with me, Peter?' she asked. 'It's *Human Desire*.'

'I'd love to,' I said. 'I haven't seen it before.'

At the end of the screening she was asked to answer questions for the students. I could see that she was uneasy. An eager-looking student stood up to pose his question. As an actress who had worked with directors like Fritz Lang, Dmytryk, Minnelli And De Mille, he asked, in her considered opinion, what was the difference between a good director and a bad director? Gloria's face turned white.

'Well,' she said after a long silence and a lot of dubious looks. 'I guess a good director's a good director and a bad director's a bad one.'

She laughed along with everyone else, and the rest of the session was a success.

Walking home later that afternoon, Gloria became unusually quiet.

'Hey, Peter. Can I ask you something?' she said, as we were halfway along Prince Albert Road. 'How do I join the Royal Shakespeare Company? I wanna play Juliet.'

'Don't be soft,' I said. 'You'd be better off playing the nurse.'

I thought I knew her well enough to make a silly joke, but it backfired. Gloria was furious.

'Dammit!' she shouted. 'How do I join the Royal Shakespeare Company? I wanna see if they think I can play those parts.'

'Well maybe you could join the RSC,' I said, trying to placate her. 'It's a good idea, but I don't think that you'd be quite right to play Juliet. That's all I mean.'

We'd just reached the entrance to the zoo when she turned on me.

'That's what it is, isn't it, Peter? Now I know why you don't like me. You just think that I'm too old. That's why you don't want to get real close. You think that I'm just an old lady. Well you're wrong. I'm gonna go to that theatre right now and I'm gonna see one of their shows. I have to take a look at the competition!'

Gloria stormed off and hailed a taxi.

Suddenly it dawned upon me why she was so mad. Gloria didn't really think that she could actually play Juliet. It was just her crazy way of trying to find out if I was sexually attracted to her.

Of course I was. The attraction was undeniable. Since the day she'd borrowed my shirt there had been many occasions when our friendship could have become closer, but I was wary of becoming involved. Gloria was a Hollywood star, she'd been married four times, and she was more than twenty years older than me. I went back home to think.

It was late. I was sitting reading when I heard footsteps running up to my room.

'Guess where I've been, Peter?' Gloria burst through the door with a triumphant look all over her face.

'The Royal Shakespeare Company,' I confidently replied.

'Well,' she said. 'I sat next to some dame in the theatre who told me that she'd played Juliet at the Royal Shakespeare Company. She'd played lots of parts there. What's more, she's a hell of a lot older than me.'

'Who was that?' I asked.

'Peggy Ashcroft,' she announced.

We collapsed in a heap of laughter on my bed.

She spent the night in my room. From then on we were inseparable.

'You're wanted on the phone! It's your cousin. It's Eileen Connolly.'

I woke up instantly. One eye opened but the other was stuck.

Eileen had a peculiar knack of 'being there' at very crucial times. It was she who, when I was thirteen years old, taught me how to smoke. Then six months later she told me about sex. She'd been my bringer of knowledge, my confidante and confessor. Her sudden appearances usually heralded a major change in my life.

'Where is she?'

'She's on the phone,' Jessie replied.

'No. *Where* is she? Tell her I'll call her back.'

'You can't. She says she wants you *now*.'

I pulled on a pair of jeans, then stumbled along the landing. As I looked down the staircase to Gloria's room I could see that the door was firmly shut, so I went into the sitting room and picked up the receiver.

'What are you doing in bed at this hour? It's nearly twelve o'clock.'

'I didn't realize. How are you?'

'Great. But listen, how are you? Jessie's just told me Gloria isn't well and that she's there with you in the house. Is that right?'

'Yes, that's right.'

'You know, it's really strange, Pete, but I've been thinking about her all week. Honest. I have. Now isn't that weird?'

'Yes, that's strange.'

'I've even had those photographs developed. Do you remember? The ones we took in New York. Oh, there's a lovely one of you and Gloria standing by the window in her flat, and there's a smashing one of me holding her Oscar. Everyone says I look like Jane Fonda, but me mother thinks I look more like Henry. All the girls at work want to have it blown up to stick behind the bar. Only for a laugh. Don't you think that's funny?'

'Eileen, I'm not properly awake. Can I call you back? I haven't yet been in to see Gloria.'

'Hang on a minute, Pete. You can't go in to see Gloria because the doctor's there with her. He's giving her an examination. Him and your mother are attending to her right now.

73

Well, that's what Jessie just told me. What's the matter with her? Is it something serious?'

'I'll have to phone you back. I'll have to see what's happening.'

'You'll have to calm down. What you need is a break. You need to get out of that house for a while. Listen, I'm working tonight at the Belgrave Club. Why don't you get yourself down there after your play and we'll be able to have a drink and a talk? That's what you need.'

'Okay, I'll see what I can do.'

'Peter,' Jessie whispered from the bottom of the stairs as I was about to go into the middle room. 'Don't go in there. Not just yet. The doctor doesn't want to be disturbed. Come down. I've made a pot of tea.'

Reluctantly I followed Jessie to the kitchen.

'What's going on? What's happened to Gloria? Why didn't you wake me up?'

'Nothing's happened. Everything's still the same.' Jessie pulled up the flaps of a carton of milk, only from the wrong end. 'Oh look what I've gone and done,' she said and wiped away the splash. 'It's just that the doctor came round again to visit Gloria and we didn't think to wake you. Anyway, we thought you needed the sleep.'

'How long has he been here?' I asked.

'Oh, not long. It can't be more than half an hour. Don't be so agitated. Sit down and have a drink of tea.'

I sat on the edge of a chair and leant my elbows on the table.

'Oh, I forgot,' Jessie said. 'You like a mug, don't you? I've gone and poured a cup.'

'That doesn't matter, I don't care what I have.'

The electric bulb, hanging from the ceiling in a plastic shade, threw out a dull white light. Carrier bags stuffed with sheets and towels, and a bundle of clothes on the floor in the corner, were waiting to go to the launderette. The sink was piled with dishes, mostly cups and saucers, needing to be washed. The room looked miserable, I thought.

'Everything's a bit of a mess,' I said.

'Now, eh.' Jessie pointed at me with a spoon. 'I've been awake all night and your mother's been up since five. Joe hasn't slept much either but he's had to go and see how things are at work. We're all a bit tired to say the least. Anyway, you look a bit of a mess yourself. If I was you I'd have a bath.'

'You're right. I think that's what I'll do.'

Jessie was standing with her coat on when I returned from taking my bath. My mother was sitting with her head down, one hand holding her forehead, the other clutching an airmail letter. Their conversation faded as I entered the room.

'It'll be all right.' I heard Jessie murmur. Then she turned to me and said, 'Your mother's got word from Billy in Australia. It's about the final arrangements.'

'That's good, isn't it?' I smiled across at my mother. 'At last you're definitely going.'

'I'm saying nothing,' my mother announced and put the letter behind the clock. 'Not until everything's been sorted out in this house. I've waited sixteen years to go on this holiday! I've waited sixteen years to see my son! All this has put the mockers on the lot. Now I won't be going anywhere.'

'Of course you will. Gloria's sister will be getting here soon. She'll help to work things out.'

'Let's see her get here first. If it was my sister I would have been here from the start.'

She started sorting through the bundle of clothes on the floor, separating the coloureds into a black plastic bag.

'The doctor's just gone. We couldn't call you because you were in the bath.' Jessie attempted to change the subject. 'But he's coming back later today.'

'What did he have to say?' I asked.

'I'll tell you what he had to say.' My mother stood up and dropped the black plastic bag to the floor. Surrounded by dirty clothes, she stood indomitable in the centre of the room. 'He's never known anything like it in his life! Hollywood's got nothing on this,' she cried and threw her hands in the air. 'I feel as though I'm living in a picture – and I've got the lousy part.' She hauled up the black plastic bag with one arm and started up the steps to the hall. 'I'm going round to the wash-house. I've had enough of this place for today.'

'I'll follow you on,' Jessie said. 'I'll bring the other bags.'

'Will you do something for me, Son?' My mother paused at the top of the steps and looked me clear in the eye. 'I want you to phone Billy and tell him I won't be coming.'

'I think that you were right, Peter,' Jessie said as my mother left the house. 'This is a terrible mess. You'd better phone Gloria's sister in California to find out when she'll arrive.'

'It's early morning there. Anyway, she's promised to call me back.'

'What's wrong with you? Worrying about waking people up, while we're all going demented.' She picked up the rest of the washing. 'And I don't think you should go up to Gloria because she needs to be left alone. The doctor says she needs to be kept quiet and not get too excited. She's losing all her body fluids. There's nothing you can do.'

Jessie followed after my mother, leaving me alone.

The most practical thing I could do for the moment, I thought, was to wash the dirty dishes. So I started with the cups. While my hands were immersed in hot water and my head was bent over the sink, I sensed that someone was look-ing at me. I peered out of the window across towards the tree and saw my father in the garden, halfway along the cement path he'd laid, and with one arm holding on to the washing line which my mother had strung above it. He stood there motionless, staring, watching me watching him.

'What are you doing out there?' I asked as I opened the back door. 'It's cold. Why don't you come inside?'

'Oh, don't mind me,' he replied. 'I'm just passing away the time.'

Pre-occupied, he didn't look at me while we spoke. His eyes still focused on the kitchen window.

'What are you looking at?'

'Your ma,' he said. 'I'm trying to see your ma.'

'She's not in here. She's just gone around to the launder-ette.'

'You don't say.' He slowly rubbed his hands together as if

making a major decision. ''E' y'are,' he said. 'Come and give me a hand with this.'

A smile spread across his face and, showing no sign of his seventy-four years, he darted along the path and disappeared around the side of the house.

'I found this along the street,' he said when I joined him by the bins. 'It was lying on its side in front of an empty house. Somebody must have thrown it away.'

'It's a bit big,' I said. 'And me mam will go mad if you bring anything else into the house. She's only just got rid of that fish tank you found.'

'Ah, well, that's because the goldfish died on account of the rusty frame, and she doesn't like to see anything dead. But look at this. Isn't it a smasher?'

Sitting on top of the kennel which Candy never used was a very old-fashioned television. About four foot high in a dark wooden frame, it had a knob at either side and a green tinted screen.

'What are you going to do with this?' I laughed. 'It can't be any good.'

'Grab hold of that end,' he said. 'Let's take it down to the stores.'

The stores, my father's den in the cellar, is where he keeps his junk – a fascinating collection of useless discarded objects. While he fiddled about with the television trying to make it work, I took the opportunity to have a look around.

Some things I remembered from different times in my childhood, while others, probably picked up on his wanderings about the streets, were new to me. In a corner was a lawn mower which I'd never seen before. Next to it was 'the roller' which my father invented when I was at school. I helped him fill the empty oil barrel with concrete and watched while, somehow, he attached to it the handle bars from a broken down old bike. Meant to flatten the soil after the garden had been turned over, it was never a success because it was too heavy to push about.

At the far end were shelves lined with paint tins, boxes and jars containing screws, nuts, bolts and a variety of used nails. Lots of bits of clocks, waiting to be put together, were scattered over a table in the middle of the room. A tea chest marked 'Shoes' and another marked 'Toys' were stacked against the wall. Another with 'Records' clearly written on the top contained only a handful of dusty books.

Hanging from a gas pipe in the ceiling was a lampshade called 'Niagara' which an uncle brought home from sea. At one time it revolved around a bulb, illuminating an endless running stream.

'I don't know why you hoard all this crap. It should all be thrown away.'

'Just pass me that torch,' he said. 'It's on the shelf above your head.'

In his cap, lying beside him on the floor, was an odd assortment of tools. He'd taken the cover off the back of the played-out television, and with a screwdriver was poking about inside.

'What are you trying to do? You'll never get it to work.'

'I wouldn't be too sure about that,' he said, and gave me a word of advice: 'If you can get a light on at the back then you know you're in with a chance. All you need is a spark.'

Just then I heard the telephone ringing, so I dashed to the

staircase which leads up to the hall. Candy, who followed behind, got stuck around my feet. Not understanding the reason for my impatience, she scrambled behind a table then ran back down to my dad.

'Hello!' I shouted through the squeaks and crackles of a transatlantic delay. 'Is that Joy?'

'Oh my God. Are you all right?'

'Yes,' I answered through the echo.

'You sound in distress.'

'I'm out of breath,' I told her. 'I've been down in the stores.'

'Oh that's awful,' she said. 'But listen, I have bad news for you. I can't come. I can't come to London.'

Throughout the explaining and regretting I stood gazing out of the window wondering what on earth I was to do. The only person who I thought might have any real practical influence over Gloria's immediate fate, her sister Joy, was now telling me that she couldn't come to England. My mother would find it hard to understand that Joy, who was a Canadian citizen, was worried about leaving America in case she was never allowed to return. Joy's worries were quite genuine but I knew my mother would think it a lame excuse, part of an absurd plot designed to prevent her from going to Australia, an event she'd planned and dreamed about for sixteen years. How could she comprehend? Why should she? I was caught between two strong and powerful women: one on the point of going to the other side of the world, the other on the verge of leaving it.

'I'm trying to contact my father, Peter,' Paulette's voice suddenly broke in. 'I need to get some money from him and then I'm flying to England. My brother might come with me. I just want to be with Mom as soon as possible. Tell her I love her and I miss her. I just have to get the air ticket from my father. He's in New York right now. I have to find out his hotel.'

While Paulette gave me messages to pass on to her mother, my attention was drawn to the view outside on the street. Joe, Jessie and my mother were standing talking at the gate. When I saw them marching up the path I hurriedly brought the conversation to a close, and prepared myself to break the latest news.

'What are you going to have? Sausages and bacon or just bacon with your egg?'

I spied through the crack of the open door to try and judge the mood in the kitchen.

Thoughtfully, Joe looked up from his newspaper, while Jessie poured the tea.

'I'm not sure if I fancy an egg,' he said.

'Oh, I've cracked it now.' My mother stood over the frying pan holding on to a broken shell. 'Someone will have to have the egg.'

'I'll have it,' I said, realizing this was the moment to join them, and sat opposite my brother at the table.

'Well, I haven't seen you eat since Monday.' My mother threw a glance in my direction. 'I'm glad. I'll fry you a few sausages as well.'

I smiled to show my enthusiasm but I wasn't in the least bit hungry.

'They're good those sausages from Tesco's,' Jessie said as she unpacked the rest of the groceries. 'I always keep a few packets in the freezer.'

'That's what I'm after.' My mother wiped the hair from the side of her face. 'One of those fridge-freezers. But look at me. I'm seventy years of age and I haven't even got an electric kettle!'

'You didn't take long at the launderette,' I said, trying to keep the conversation chatty.

'We left it in for a service,' Jessie explained. 'It's only thirty pence. I wanted to be here for Joe, and your mother's got a pain in her back.'

'A pain in the back' I knew to be a serious subject so I diverted the attention to the dog.

'Candy. Come on, Candy,' I called.

'Oh eh,' Joe said and protected his bacon butty. 'Do we have to have the dog around the table?'

Candy hung her head and wedged herself under my chair. Joe went back to his food, Jessie put the shopping into the larder and my mother stood over the stove. Except for the sausages sizzling away in the pan, the room was silent. On the surface, the tension had relaxed but, for me, the pressure was mounting. I had to explain to my mother that Joy wasn't able to come. To upset her any further was more than I could bear.

'Has that dog been fed?' she inquired as she put the sausages and egg before me.

Candy, wearing a look that undoubtedly said 'No', dragged herself up from the floor and wagged over to her bowl.

'Everything's left to me,' my mother sighed as she knelt to get the dog food from its place beneath the sink. 'This should be a job for your father.' As she opened the cupboard the door fell off its hinge. 'Oh I'm sick of it. I am. I'm bloody sick of it.' She pulled away the broken door and threw it on the floor. 'Another man wouldn't let me suffer like this. He doesn't give a shite. I don't know what possessed me to marry him.'

'It's a bit late to wonder about that,' Joe tried to make her laugh. 'You've been married for fifty years. That's why you're going to Australia.'

'Now that's where you're wrong.' She turned on Joe and emphasized each word with the point of her finger. The movement of her hands and shoulders suggested all her feeling. There was a definite change of mood. 'I won't be going anywhere. I'm going to call the whole thing off.'

'Now that's not right. It's not right on them, they've made arrangements for you to be there. You can't tell them the week before you're supposed to go that you won't be coming. Anyway, I don't believe you,' he said. 'I don't believe that you don't want to go.'

'Look, Joe. I know. You're right. You don't have to tell me nothing. I just want you all to listen to me for a change. I'm the mother of this house. It's about time that I got to be a bit more integrated with what's happening here.' She paused to collect her thoughts, then took her place at the head of the table. She spoke in sombre tones. 'I wouldn't go away and leave a dying woman in one of my bedrooms. My conscience wouldn't allow me to do a thing like that. Gloria is critically ill and I don't understand why nobody seems to want to do a thing about it. She's just left upstairs to fade and I think that's a disgrace.'

'I agree with you, Mother. You're absolutely right. Gloria's about to die. She's refused to go to a hospital, she doesn't even want the doctor, but she is, so we've been told, going into a coma. So when that happens we'll just have to . . .'

'Oh stop it, Joe. Stop it. All of you just stop it.' Jessie sat down tearful at the table. 'I don't like to hear you all talking about Gloria like that.'

'There's no other way we can talk, love. I think it's tragic. I think it's horrible and I think it's awful, but that's the situation. Very soon it will all be over. Until then we've got to try and be practical. Peter,' he turned to me. 'What about her sister? When will she arrive?'

I looked down at my egg and then I broke the yolk.

'She can't come,' I said. 'Joy phoned to say she can't come.'

It took about three or four seconds for the information to be absorbed, then my mother pulled her hands to her head and let out a terrible moan.

'That's it! THAT IS JUST ABOUT IT! I'm going to phone that sister right now. It won't take me five minutes to hand out my medical bulletin. Why won't nobody realize that that woman upstairs is dying? I'm going to phone America!'

'Paulette's coming instead,' I weakly tried to explain.

'When?' my mother demanded. 'When? Tell me when.'

'When she gets the air fare from her dad.'

'That's enough! Now I've had enough!' The chair was pushed aside as my mother threw herself up from the table. The sugar bowl crashed to the floor and shattered into pieces. 'I'm going to phone for the ambulance,' she shouted. 'I'm taking poor Gloria to the hospital now!'

Hysteria suddenly exploded. Joe blocked my mother's

path as she lunged across the room, and Jessie got squashed between. Candy ran around in circles and barked at the top of her voice. Pandemonium let loose. The kitchen was in uproar as Gloria appeared from the hall.

The horror of the moment suspended all reality. It was as if we were turned to stone.

Wraith-like, in a long white nightdress and with her hair hanging limp around her face, she looked bewilderedly about the room. She struggled to control her breath and speak. When she did, a calm descended. Gloria was serene.

'Look at me. I'm not sick. I'm not gonna die.' She appealed to each of us in turn. 'Why are you talking about me? I can hear you through the floor.'

'Oh Gloria, love,' my mother said, all the anger had melted away. 'Let Peter help you to the warm.'

'She's a star! She's a movie star! Take her out the back way. She can't be seen drunk!'

We were deaf to our host the night we were high on champagne. Because of eager photographers waiting at the door, we were advised to leave the party without being noticed.

Proud and defiant, we held each other tight and slowly groped and picked our way up the steep flight of stairs until we reached the top. Gloria was determined to leave the party the same way as she came.

Memory of that night in New York came hurtling into my mind as I took Gloria up to the middle room. She fought every inch of the way. She was happy with her achievement. She was pleased with what she'd done.

'I've made it down the stairs and back again,' she held on

to me in triumph. 'I'm getting better, Peter. I must be getting better.'

I carried her into the room and sat her on the bed.

I handed her the piece of broken mirror and then the green plastic wash-bag. I opened up the window and then I closed the curtains. I switched on the table lamp and put it on the floor. I did everything she asked. I did everything I could.

Then, when she turned to face me, the shadows re-appeared; Gloria had put on her make-up. The browns and the greens were smudged; the red was on a slant. It was too late to attempt a rescue. Nothing could have helped her. Not even a pale pink light.

'Tell me, Peter. Tell me. Tell me how I look.'

I told her she was beautiful.

FOUR

Old Jack was in his cubby hole listening to the radio; his assistant stage manager was doing all the hard work, setting up the props for the play. All the actors, except Geoffrey, were hanging about in the Green Room. Gil, dressed in her first-act costume, her hair pinned back from her face which hadn't yet been covered by the mask of stage make-up, was talking on the telephone. She gave me a friendly wave. I smiled and she blew me a kiss. Eric, sitting in the corner, was chewing on a double giant hamburger from the stall across the street. While Linda, happily wearing nothing much at all, except a towel and her sloppy silver shoes, was pinning up a notice in the centre of the board. 'Rave Up' it announced, 'chez moi, Huskisson Street. Bring yourself something to drink'.

At least everything was normal in the world of make-believe. Tonight it was a relief to be at the theatre. As soon as I was involved in my performance I felt immune to what was happening at home. I was tired, I was drained, but strangely I didn't feel lacking in energy while I was on stage; it was only after the play was over that I felt exhausted and low.

'Are you going to Linda's party?' Gil, back in her everyday clothes, popped her head around the dressing room door.

'No, I'm not,' I told her.

'Oh, don't be so miserable. You can't just go back home.'

No, I can't, I thought. I couldn't face going back to the house. I needed a break. I decided to go and see my cousin Eileen at the Belgrave Club.

Eileen was the only person with whom I felt I could relax. Ever since I'd spoken to her earlier in the day I'd been thinking about what she had said. She was right, I needed to calm down. For a while, I had to get away from the sadness in the house.

I took a taxi from Clayton Square. It smelt of cigarettes and chips, which made me feel an emptiness inside. We drove up London Road, away from the down-town area, where anything that might happen, could happen. Ten minutes later we drew up outside the Belgrave. To me it seemed an odd place for a gambling club, standing isolated, alone, in the middle of a wasteland. It looked a bit of a dump.

As I wasn't a member, and I didn't look as if I was dressed for a night out in a casino, the two big bouncers sentried at the door refused to let me in.

'If you've been invited, why hasn't yer name been put on the list?' the ugliest one of them asked.

'Because it's my cousin,' I pleaded. 'She's a pip boss, you know, a croupier. She just asked me to come along.'

Eventually, after a check upstairs with Eileen and a warning that I wasn't to sit at the tables, I was led upstairs.

Inside it was quite smart and much bigger than I'd imagined it to be. Gloria would have approved of the subdued lighting that attracted a thin smoky cloud. The atmosphere was pleasant and friendly. The punters, a regular-looking crowd, were quiet and intent. All conversations were kept to a minimum. The only noises came from the waitresses serving drinks, from the turn of the roulette wheel, and from the counting of chips being stacked on the tables.

Eileen was sitting high up on a stool at the far end of the room watching over a game. Wearing an elegant black dress and with her hair twisted up at the back, she looked very glamorous in her 'Solitaire' pose, which came slightly unstuck as she spotted me at the door. Her face lit up and burst into a familiar smile as I walked across the casino to get to her. Wearing jeans and my old worn-out overcoat, I felt awkward and embarrassed in this sacred atmosphere, but as I reached my cousin she put her hand out to touch my arm.

'I'll join you at the bar in about five minutes. I'll take a bit of a break then,' she spoke to me in a whisper, then turned her attention back to the cards. 'The twenty-five pound bet goes for the next hand,' she quietly told the dealer, but in a louder voice called after me, 'The girl behind the bar's called Debbie.'

A dispute arose at the table between the dealer and a suspicious-looking punter, and as I made my way over to the bar I could hear my cousin say, 'I'm sorry, sir. The twenty-five-pound chip was a late bet. I can't let that pass.'

Debbie was counting cigarettes in a packet.

'I've only had five today!' she told me in her sing-song Liverpool accent. 'That's good, isn't it? Do you want one? I'm not supposed to smoke working behind the bar, but it's quiet tonight.'

I took a cigarette and Debbie struck a match.

'Thanks,' I said and propped myself up against the counter.

'Now why don't you take that big overcoat off?' She took a quick succession of puffs then sent the smoke into the air.

'It's nice and warm in here. Anyway, you won't feel the benefit of it once you get back outside.'

'You're Debbie,' I said by way of introduction.

'You're right,' she replied and gave me a flirtatious look. 'You can have what you want to drink.'

'I think I'll have a Scotch.' I reached for the money in my pocket.

'Oh don't be soft,' Debbie pushed herself close to the other side of the bar. 'Put your money away, Eileen's told me not to charge. You're her cousin, aren't yer? I heard you might come in. Your name's Peter, isn't it? And yer an actor, aren't yer? You look different from how I imagined you to be. I thought you were blond and blue, not dark and going thin. Still, I won't allow the superficials to – affect me strong emotion. You can have ice in that drink if you want, or else there's water in that jug.'

Debbie told me she was all of twenty-three. Her hourglass figure was squeezed into complementing clothes. She was stunning. In between giggles she told me about herself.

'I'm an actress. Well, I've got me Equity card. I used to dance in a club with a snake called Emma but I'm not doing that any more. I left her in a vanity case on the bus, so I got the sack. I'm just working here for the money. I want to go to Hollywood and be a movie star.' She took away my glass and poured me another huge Scotch. 'Here's your Eileen coming over. I want her to see that I'm looking after you properly.'

'Ahhh, it's great to see you.' Eileen gave me an affectionate hug. 'I'm glad you could manage to come. Now look, Pete, I've only got a few minutes break and then I'm back on duty, but only for half an hour. Then we can pop. I've asked Carol to take over the tables for me and she says she doesn't mind. So when I finish work we'll go back down into town to an after-hours Chinese club called the Oceania. It's a nice place, small, so we can talk and have a couple of drinks. Listen, I'll have to get back to the tables now, but Debbie will look after you. And don't worry about money. This place takes lots of cash.'

She hurried back to her stool overlooking the tables while Debbie sashayed her way to serve a customer at the far end of the bar.

'Cocktails. Cocktails. Good luck to you, sir.'

The girls were very attractive. I guessed they were probably show girls who had been in too many different shows and just got stuck out in the desert.

The whole feeling of Vegas was one of dice and vice. Soon after we arrived at the airport the first thing I noticed was a hooker. Then rows and rows of one-armed bandits.

I'd just finished work on a play in England and had flown out to be with Gloria who was finishing work on a film. The location setting was Las Vegas, Nevada; the place where fortunes have been made one night and gambled away the next.

It was late afternoon when we arrived. By the time we reached the hotel, driving past all the glossy hoardings announcing the famous names who were appearing there – Anthony Newley, Carol Channing, Juliet Prowse and the like – it was dark, and the whole of the strip was lit up in fantastic neon.

One of the more excessive illuminations was a huge silver slipper set with multi-coloured lights and suspended in the sky.

The lobby of the hotel was not simply a reception area but a vast assembly of gaming tables surrounded by hordes of delighted or disillusioned faces; the courtiers of Caesar in his tinsel palace.

As the primary pursuit in Las Vegas was to gamble, Gloria and I decided to chance our luck. We pulled at every slot machine in sight that promised a million dollars and one night we played blackjack until the early morning light. We were caught in an exciting compulsive trap.

Gloria got taken up by an admirer who showed us around the town. He was a small-time professional gambler who worked as a film extra whenever the going was rough. He claimed to have appeared in over a hundred movies and at one time he owned a big ranch. Max knew Las Vegas like the dealers knew the dollars; he arranged for us to see all the big shows.

The Folies de Paris was a great extravaganza and the MGM show was indeed grand, but the evening with Raquel Welch was particularly spectacular. The curtain went up on Ms Welch standing at the top of the biggest staircase I'd seen. She then proceeded to walk down it while singing 'You've either got it or you ain't'. By the time she reached the bottom and had finished her song, it was quite clear to everyone that she had everything anybody would ever wish to have.

'It's all surgery,' somebody said when there was a lull in the thunderous applause.

'I don't believe that,' Gloria objected. 'That simply could not be true.' Then she leant close to my ear and whispered. 'But if that's the case, as soon as I get back to New York I'm gonna have surgery too!'

Later we dined at a Japanese restaurant which looked like the peak on Mount Fuji. To the strains of piped Nippon muzak, we crossed a bridge over an oriental babbling brook and were seated at a table three feet off the floor. Scalding towels, geisha girls, samurai and lanterns were extras on the menu, but we did not get around to those. When Gloria was recognized by a posse of gangsters playing with their chopsticks and New Jersey broads, she decided it was time to leave.

'I don't wanna get wrapped up with any gangsters,' she said when we got to the door. 'I met one once who gave me diamonds but I sent them back. I didn't wanna end up in the East River.'

We went back to flutter away our two dollar chips at the blackjack and drink the free drinks handed out by the cocktail girls.

'Another large Scotch for yer thoughts! You're awful serious aren't yer?'

'Thanks, Debbie. I'm sorry. I was just thinking about someone I know.'

'Oh well, maybe you ought to think about somebody else.' She ran her hands around the curves of her body and gave me a sexy wink.

The club was starting to fill up now. More people were crowding around the gaming tables and a group of flash Greek gangster boys came and sat around the bar. A roar of approval came from the direction of the craps table, for some high roller the dice were very hot, and a lecherous laugh erupted from the gangsters as Debbie reached for a glass.

'Oh I'm glad that's over with,' Eileen said when she joined

me. 'I'm absolutely shattered. That bastard at the blackjack table tried to pull every trick in the book.' She frowned. 'But he knows that I'm on to him,' she added with a glint in her eye. 'I bet he hates me guts. Anyway, let's get out of this place. I'm gasping for a ciggy and a drink. Let's pop. I've just got to pick up me things.'

I followed her to a room which had 'Private' written on the door. Dominated by a blinking fluorescent strip, it was narrow and small. A formica-topped table supported a redundant Kenco coffee machine; a mound of handbags, umbrellas and coats were piled up on a cupboard; a few drinking glasses, saucers and cups, some full of cigarette ash and stubs, were on a tray in the middle of the floor, and three high metal bar stools were shoved against the wall.

A young man, one of the croupiers, was slouched in an armchair watching television in the corner. The picture was snowy and the volume too loud.

'Pete, this is Kenneth, Kenneth, this is Peter.'

Kenneth looked forlorn. His face was pale and gaunt and, judging by the way the pupils of his eyes seemed to revolve, I imagined that he worked the roulette.

While Eileen found her coat and got herself ready to leave, I sat on one of the stools and leant my head against the wall, feeling sweaty and claustrophobic. I was glad when it was time to 'pop'.

'Eh, don't forget this,' Debbie shouted as we passed through the bar on our way out of the club, 'or you'll have nothing to keep away the cold.' She ran around from behind the counter and threw me my old overcoat.

'Thanks, Debbie, thanks for the drinks. I hope I see you again.'

'You never know yer luck,' she said as she shimmied away.

It was after midnight by the time we left the casino but there was no shortage of taxis waiting outside for a fare.

'Chinatown,' Eileen told the driver. 'Just on the corner by the Blackie.'

The Blackie, an old abandoned church, signposts the boundary of Liverpool's dwindling Chinese community. Chinatown is, and always has been, a lively and colourful part of the city.

At the turn of the century, when Liverpool was a major sea port, its Chinese population became one of the biggest in Europe. It didn't take long before good and inexpensive hand laundry businesses sprang up all over the place. Exotic restaurants opened and chop suey rolls or chicken chow mein and rice became an alternative to fish and chips. Now times have changed. The city is broke and has one of the highest unemployment figures in the land. Few Liverpudlians can afford to send their washing to the laundry so most of the Chinese laundries have had to close down. Not many people have the money to eat in fancy restaurants, and even fish and chips have been hit by a ridiculous tax. Politicians have allowed the heart of the city to be ripped apart, and Liverpool has lost most of its beauty and character as well as some of its Chinese inhabitants. But those Chinese who do remain are completely at home with the Scouse sense of humour and style.

The taxi put us off at the corner of Duke Street and Nelson Street, just across the road from the Blackie. We walked around the corner to the Oceania, knocked at the door and had to wait for a few minutes before we were allowed in.

Pictures and mirrors covered the walls in the hallway and a flowery-patterned carpet ran the length of the stairs. It was just like somebody's house until we got to the landing on the fourth floor where Sonny was sitting on a desk outside a curtain-covered door. More Liverpudlian than Chinese in mannerisms and speech, he was young, attractive and friendly.

'It should be fifty pence to get in,' he said. 'But forget the cash, just sign the book.' He pulled back the curtain, opened the door and ushered us into the club.

Suddenly we were in the centre of a dance floor and were plunged into what seemed like total darkness until the revolving glitter ball hanging from the ceiling showered us with sparkles: we were blinded by the dark and then the light. I narrowly avoided walking between two girls who were shuffling around their handbags to the sound of Roberta Flack . . . 'The first time ever I saw your face' . . . then Eileen directed me beyond the dance floor to the main room of the club which had tables and chairs spread out like a fan around a brightly lit bar in the corner. We sat at a table in a recess, cut off at either side from the other customers but with an open view of the dancers. The music was at a comfortable level which allowed us to talk without having to shout.

'Christ, Pete. After listening to that story you've just told me in that taxi, I definitely need a drink. I'm in a state of shock. No wonder you look depressed. I know, let's light that candle.'

She pulled across a candle which was standing in an aluminium ashtray and put a light to the wick. It flickered for a moment before we were protected by the glow.

'That's better,' she said. 'There's something very reassuring about that little light.'

The Chinese waiter who came over yawned as he handed us the menu, then apologized profusely.

'Oh stay, stay,' he insisted. 'Don't go. Everything you want to drink.'

Eileen smiled to show *she* understood.

'Ah,' she said. 'I know how you must feel, lad. I have to work nights.' Then she turned to me, but spoke to him. 'Let's have a nice bottle of the house red wine.'

He hurried away and within seconds returned with two glasses and a bottle.

'It'll do,' Eileen said quietly as she handed me a glass.

I took a sip. The 'wine' tasted more like whisky.

'Well,' she said, after knocking back her drink. 'Let's talk.'

I drank my glass of wine.

'Jessie told me on the phone that Gloria was sick but honest, Pete, I didn't think for a minute that it was that bad. I can't believe it. I just can't believe that she's dying. Oh,' she said and clasped her hands to her mouth. 'I wish I'd never told you about those photographs I took of us all in New York.'

'No, I'm glad you did,' I said and poured another drink. 'I want to see them.'

'Oh Peter, there's one of Gloria in a T-shirt and shorts looking wonderful, just wonderful, and that wasn't too long ago. She doesn't look ill at all. I remember, I'd only met her for a few minutes and when I told her that I used to be a hairdresser she dragged me to the bathroom and wanted me to make her look like Bo Derek. I just covered her head with masses of Carmen rollers, but it looked nice though, didn't it?'

'Yes,' I said. 'She looked fabulous.'

Eileen sighed, opened her bag and took out a photograph from between the pages of her address book. She glanced at it before she handed it to me.

Crumpled in Kodacolour, arms wrapped about each other, laughing faces pushed together, there was Gloria, there we were, standing on the corner of Central Park West.

'Fabulous,' I repeated. 'Gloria looks just fabulous.'

'Ah, it's such a shame.' Eileen put her hand out to take hold of mine. 'Such a terrible shame, and she's nice. I remember that day,' she added and took away the snap. 'I'd been so miserable on that bleeding ship. There's nothing so boring as being a croupier on a cruise. Though we were only docking there for a day, I couldn't wait to get to New York. It was just wonderful sailing up the Hudson River, saying hello to the Statue of Liberty, and going past all those big skyscrapers. I knew you'd be in one of them; even though I didn't get an answer from me letter, I just knew that you'd be in one of them big buildings looking out the window, waiting for my ship. "Just peel the portholes with your eyelashes," I said to the girls, "our Peter'll be waiting for me at the bottom of the plank," and there you were, you and Gloria. I couldn't believe it. Fancy arriving in America and being welcomed by a movie star! I just couldn't believe it. Neither could the girls – jealous snatches they were. But anyway –' she smiled and her eyes lit up with excitement – 'I had a fabulous time. We went shopping at Bloomingdales. And we went to Macy's. I'll never forget that Macy's. Remember?'

I remembered.

'We had champagne and we had oysters at Grand Central Station . . .'

It was hot. The city was beginning to bake. Even the nightmare sounds from sirens in cars were muffled by the heat; dwellers on steps, with their music, blasted the ghettos; cops chewing gum hung around the sidewalks bartering with crime; athletes on skates livened up the traffic; narcotics adorned the corner of 42nd Street. New York was on parade.

Since our first meeting in May, 1978, Gloria and I had been living under the same roof, on and off, for over two years. By this time, August 1980, the relationship had taken on a permanency which had been unexpected, but nice. We had made each other laugh; we'd become friends and then lovers. She'd made several visits to Liverpool, which she loved, and had met most of my brothers and sisters, whom she adored; especially Joe and Jessie with whom we'd been on holiday to a cottage in the mountains in Wales.

I'd been to her apartment in New York for a short time the year before, and I'd also visited her in California while she'd been working on a film. Her career had been going great and mine was picking up. I'd just finished working in the theatre, and a film of *The Tempest*, which I'd acted in, had recently been released. Gloria had been particularly busy and was continually back and forth across the Atlantic. We'd reached a point in our relationship where, if it were to continue, we had to sit down and give serious thought to the question of where we were going to live.

'I've got it!' Gloria had been 'thinking' hard for a long time one day. 'I have a big old empty apartment in Manhattan. Why don't we just go there?'

'I'm not sure that I want to actually move to America,' I hesitated.

'Well, if you don't like it you can always move back. Come on, Peter. Don't be a spoil sport. Give it a try.'

A few days later we set up home together in the apartment on the twenty-fifth floor.

I loved it. There was a never ending list of things to do in New York. We fixed up the apartment, did a bit of decorating and bought a few more pieces of furniture, mostly from the second-hand stores up and down 9th Avenue. Scouring the junk shops for bargains was one of Gloria's favourite hobbies; her prize purchase was a beautiful 1930s' blue metal desk.

I delighted in exploring the 'Isle of Manhattan'. Not once did I feel threatened or intimidated, I felt befriended by the city, as if I were a native. I walked everywhere; just looking at the people, getting accustomed to their expressions, what they wore for clothes, their movements and their sounds. I marvelled at the technology, and the buildings, not only for their beauty, but also for sheer expanse and size; each time I went up in a lift I wondered if I might need a safety belt.

At night time we went to the movies, to the theatre, then maybe a restaurant somewhere. Otherwise we stayed at home, content with each other and, of course, our spectacular view. We were having a wonderful time.

'There's something I don't understand, Peter.' Eileen paused and drained her glass of wine. 'Gloria was looking good and riding high. You were both looking great together. I don't understand what's happened. Why didn't you know she was ill? I don't understand what's led to this.'

'I don't really understand either. It's just that one day everything turned strange.'

Gloria went out one morning saying that she had an appointment with her agent, which I found out afterwards wasn't true. When she returned a few hours later, she closed herself in her room. At first I assumed that she was just 'thinking' and would at some time confront me with some fantastical idea, so I didn't take much notice. Then after a while I started to wonder and thought that, perhaps, she was indulging in one of her childlike, petulant sulks. It was more than that; she was taken over by a heavy, morose moodiness.

We didn't go out that night as we'd planned. We hardly spoke. Gloria just wanted to be left alone; and she smoked. I'd never known her smoke so much. I remember having to go to the store across the street because she'd finished all the cigarettes.

'Do you want to go downstairs for a drink?' I suggested.

'Not tonight,' she replied.

Later, I took her in some coffee. The air was thick with smoke. Gloria was lying in the dark; I couldn't make out the look on her face; the light from around the mirror in the bathroom only just reached her black suede stilettoes, which had been kicked off at the side of the bed.

'What's up?' I turned to her and said.

'What's up!' she scowled. 'What does it mean "What's up"? You've only been in America for five minutes and you can't stop saying "What's up".'

It took about twenty-four hours for her to become more communicative, but after that day our relationship was never the same again.

Over the next few weeks she became demanding and possessive, even secretive, taking to disappearing for hours at a time without giving any clue as to where she was going. There were times when we got on well, we had fun, the relationship was like it used to be, but these instances were getting few and far between. Without any apparent reason our life together had very quickly taken a downward turn.

Throughout this time Gloria looked beautiful, radiant, and actually started to take more interest in her appearance. She even stepped up her health regime, going regularly to the gym and becoming even more 'faddy' about her food, but she smoked a lot, which was unusual for her. She actually started to buy cigarettes.

I concluded that she was either having an affair or was just fed up with me. At any rate, it was obvious that things were not working out between us, and after all, it wasn't a conventional liaison. For a start, there was the big age difference, although that had never really mattered to us before. However, Gloria was a well-known actress, she was a film star, socially sought after, other people competed for her attention.

In London, I suppose, it had been easier for us to be together. I was on home ground. She came to live in the same house as me; we became fascinated by each other; and we fell in love.

Now, in New York, things were different; our equilibrium was upset. I started to think about going home.

When my agent phoned from London one day to say that

I'd been offered a part in a television series I was delighted and relieved, and I made up my mind to leave New York as soon as I could.

The fact that I was leaving to do a job would, I thought, lessen the need for Gloria and me to face the fact that our relationship had gone very wrong; it would make the parting amiable, at least easier. Gloria would be charming and say that she was sad but pleased for me, excited that I'd got a good part. However, the night I told her I was going she got upset, she started to cry. We went out for a drink. When we got home we had a row; we had an awful row and said some terrible things to each other; jealousy and misconceptions came to the surface. The next morning I handed in my key and closed the door of the apartment on the twenty-fifth floor.

It was a very hot autumn day; I felt glad to be getting away. After locking my bags up at the East Side terminal, I went for a last look around New York. Wandering about the city I slowly started to think, trying to work out what had happened. Lunch was lonely in Greenwich Village, and walking back up town, along by the Hudson River, I felt sad.

By the middle of the afternoon, exhausted and upset, I found myself back outside the apartment block on the corner of 9th and 43rd. I dialled Gloria's number from the callbox across the street and when she picked up the receiver I said, 'It's me', but she immediately put it back down; so I got on a bus which took me to the airport and I arrived back in London the following day.

My television work took me off on location to Hong Kong. While I was there I thought about Gloria a lot, missed her, sent her several letters; but she didn't reply.

Then unexpectedly, a few months after my return, I got a letter, just a short note:

'Both Sartre and Camus said when they died that in this world there is only love that is important.'

I telephoned her but she was never at home. Then I heard that she was away somewhere, performing in a play. I contacted Paulette in California to see if she knew what had happened to her mother, but she told me that Gloria had gone to stay with friends. I left messages for her everywhere but she didn't get in touch. I assumed that she didn't want to bother with our friendship any more. That's what I thought, until I got the call from Lancaster.

The music was louder now, the club was filling up. The two girls were still shuffling around their handbags; the spotlights were changing colour to the rhythm of the music, going from red to yellow to green, just like a traffic light; the glitter ball was spinning fast; the sparkles crossed over my cousin's face.

'Why didn't she tell me, Eileen? Why didn't she tell me she was sick?'

'Maybe she just didn't want you to know.' Eileen looked at me across the dancing yellow flame.

'But I wouldn't have left her in New York. I would never have left her the way I did, I should have made her tell me what was wrong.'

'Now look, Pete, you can't blame yourself for anything that's happened, Gloria must have had her reasons for not telling you she was ill. What's happened has happened. You can't change that. Things don't always go the way you would like them to. Something will always go wrong, things will always get fucked up. Life's like that. Gloria just kept this secret, I don't know why. Anyway, let's not get depressed. Let's not get upset. Let's drink to Gloria. Let's drink to life.'

FIVE

It was a bright morning but cold. Clouds were moving fast across the sky, and before the taxi had reached the end of Prince's Avenue, five minutes away from home, specks of rain were hitting the windows of the cab.

Liverpool taxi drivers like to chat. This one was not so much talkative as poetic:

'That's right rain clouds, do your job. Bring the rain. Clean up God's land.'

At first I wasn't quite sure if he was talking to me or delivering an ode to the morning sky, so I kept quiet, deciding not to get involved. But after a few minutes' silence, and then attempts to attract my attention, he started off again.

'Don't you think it's awful? It certainly needs to be cleaned up. What do you think?'

Was he talking about Prince's Avenue? Or the state of the world? The avenue looked clean enough to me and the state of the world was more than I could cope with the way I was feeling, anxious and sick, and hungover. I wasn't in the mood for talking but the driver wasn't easily put off.

'On your way to work, are you?'

'No. I'm on my way to see someone who is very seriously ill.'

I thought that might shut him up, but it was the worst thing I could have said, for he then handed me a copy of *Watchtower*, the Jehovah's Witness newspaper. As he bombarded me with quotes from the Bible the safety of his driving seemed to suffer, so I got out of the cab at the end of the avenue, feeling it would be better to walk the rest of the way home.

The house looked tranquil from the outside. The milk had been taken in off the step and all the curtains were pulled back; that's a good sign, I thought as I opened the gate quietly and started to walk up the path.

I was feeling nervous about going in, and guilty about staying out all night: I shouldn't have drunk till four in the morning; I shouldn't have stayed the night at Eileen's; I should have been here with Gloria.

Expecting noise and activity, I was greeted by an absolute silence. No one seemed to be at home. The kitchen was empty and in darkness; the daylight was shadowed by the branches of the dangerous, threatening tree.

'I heard you get back.' My mother looked tired when she opened the door and walked the few steps down into the room. She moaned and held her back with her left hand as she went to the sink with the kettle.

'Is your back bad?' I said.

'Is it bad? It's like a knife. Just like a knife sticking right up through the ribs. There's bacon in the fridge if you want, or else have cornflakes.'

'Gloria,' I said, but I struggled for the words. 'Mum . . . is she all right?'

'Well . . .' She turned to me and sighed. 'She's been asking for you.'

Gloria was looking miserable. Her hair had been brushed back off her forehead and her face had been cleaned of lipstick and eye-shadow, leaving no trace of the hideous mask which she had painted on the previous evening. Order and sanity were restored to the room. The curtains were wide open, the window was closed and any unpleasant smell had been replaced by Dettol. The bedlinen had been changed and Gloria was wearing another of my mother's flowery nightdresses. She would be far happier in a dark and scented bedroom, wearing complete make-up, and her hair parted at the side with a wavy fringe falling over one eye.

'I want the make-up bag, Peter.' She looked at me then slowly looked away.

This was probably the worst humiliation – to be without her make-up and denied her pride and dignity.

'Why didn't you come back, Peter?'

'Because I went to see Eileen. We went to a club . . . and then it was too late.'

'Okay.' She didn't have the energy to be angry, just nodded and repeated, 'Okay. But can I have my make-up bag? It's my nails. Please, Peter, I want to clean my nails.'

'I didn't have a wink of sleep last night and neither did Gloria.' My mother was sitting alone at the kitchen table.

'I'm sorry.' Guiltily I sat down next to her. 'I'm sorry I didn't get back home.'

'Look,' there was a fixed, determined expression on her

face, 'I don't want to know where you've been or what you've been doing, but there's a few things I've got to be telling you. To begin with, I'll be looking after Gloria from now on.'

'Where's Joe and Jessie? Why aren't they here? I thought they were staying the night to help you out.'

'They would have done if they'd have known that you wouldn't be back. Anyway, they've got their own family to look after. They can't be here all the time. I don't know what you're playing at, leaving me alone to cope. Even your father's done the bunk. He left the house at half past eight to buy a new cap for Australia, now he'll be gone all day.'

'What was it you wanted to tell me?' I said.

'Right. The daughter's been on the phone. She's leaving America today. She's coming with her brother. And they'll arrive sometime tomorrow.'

'Where are they going to sleep?'

'We'll have to get a room booked for them at a hotel, there's not enough beds for them here.'

'Are you certain they're arriving tomorrow?'

'I'm certain all right. I told her if she wants to see her mother alive ever again, she'd better get here quick.'

I could see that she was relieved that Paulette and Tim would be arriving because in a strange way, for my mother, their presence would make the fact that Gloria was dying upstairs in her house more legitimate.

She was now less agitated by the trauma and confusion and started to tell me about the previous evening: Gloria had wanted to keep on her make-up; it had become smudged and dirty so my mother cleaned it off. She'd brushed back her hair and helped her into a clean nightgown. Later, during the early morning hours, Gloria had started to ramble, talking about strange things and going in and out of a trance-like state.

'What was she saying?'

'She was rambling, whispering things, asking where you were. Then she said she wanted to put on a dress.'

'Gloria doesn't like dresses!'

'Well, that's what she said. I looked through her suitcase, but she's got nothing nice with her in the way of clothes except a pair of silky pyjamas, and they need a wash. She hasn't even got a dress. Did you leave most of her clothes in Lancaster?'

'No, Mum. Gloria doesn't have many clothes.'

'The poor girl. It's breaking my heart, it is. God love her, she won't be needing them now.'

Her eyes reddened. The drama and hysteria had taken its toll; she was very upset.

My mother was fond of Gloria. I never knew how much she understood of our relationship, she never asked any questions, but the two women got on well with each other, even though they were worlds apart.

'Peter.'

'What, Mum?'

'I think we should get the priest. She's started to pick at herself.'

'What do you mean – she's started to pick at herself?'

'She's started to pick at herself, as if she's picking things off her body. They all do that just before the end. There's only a short time left for her now.'

The sound of the doorbell broke our silence.

'It'll be the doctor. I want you to stay in here,' she said, getting up to answer it. I'll take him up to Gloria. Why don't you go and book a room for Tim and Paulette in one of those hotels by the park?'

I could hear the preliminaries of conversation as my mother brought the doctor into the house.

'Isn't it awful? The weather. What a day it's turning out to be. The heavens have opened.'

'Yes, it's surprising the way things have changed over the last week, doctor. We're into October now.'

'That's right,' he said. 'We're into October. Where's the summer gone?'

Their chattering continued as they climbed up the stairs to Gloria's room. Everything went quiet except for the sound of the rain.

I stood by the window and looked out towards the tree. It looked harsh. Defiant. The wind lashed against the branches. They lurched from side to side, ducking, fighting, teasing; provoking the storm. I knew that very soon the tree would certainly fall. The rain streamed down the window clouding my view. I sat down and cried.

Bang! Bang! Bang!

'Open this bloody door.' It was Joe, angrily shouting from outside the back door.

'I'm coming,' I said and wiped my face on my sleeve.

'Oh Peter, hurry up,' Jessie shouted. 'We're soaked right through.'

I opened the door and two very wet people pushed past and ran into the house.

'Why did you come the back way?' I asked.

'Because the garden door was open, so we just ran right round, didn't we, Joe? It's raining cats and dogs.'

'And the bleeding car broke down! Just at the end of the road. That's all I need.' Joe threw off his wet jacket and sat on the steps to take off his boots.

'You look terrible, Peter.' Jessie untied her headscarf and shook it over the sink. 'Didn't you get any sleep?'

'A little bit,' I said and lit the gas under the kettle. 'I'll make you a cup of tea.'

'Well? How is Gloria?'

'She's been rambling and talking to herself.'

'What was she saying?'

'I don't know, Jessie. I wasn't here.'

'What do you mean you weren't here?' Joe's eyes narrowed on me. 'Where were you then?'

'I needed to get away. I went to see Eileen Connolly at the Belgrave.'

'Do you mean to say that you spent the night at a casino?' He was now totally fixed on me and I could feel a fury brewing.

'No, Joe. Not exactly.'

'Where did you spend it then?'

'I wanted to talk. I had to talk to Eileen. We went to a club in Chinatown.'

'Do you mean to tell me that you left Gloria upstairs in this house with no one except the old girl to look after her, while you went out drinking and spending the night on a club crawl?' Joe's body contorted into a state of absolute rage. 'I've heard some terrible things but that's the worst. You don't care about anyone except yourself. That's it with you. I don't want anything more to do with you.'

'No, it wasn't like that, Joe. I wanted to talk about Gloria. And anyway, I thought you and Jessie were here.'

'Of course you thought we'd be here. "Joe's there so he'll do my work for me. I can go out and get drunk." That's what you thought. You didn't think for one minute about Gloria and you certainly didn't care about me. I've got my own house and kids and a business to keep going, without having to take on your problems. Running you about in the car all week – that's why it's packed up now. And you don't care about that. But the worst thing is the fact that you left Gloria all night while you were out clubbing.'

'Now look, Joe,' I shouted back at him. 'It just wasn't like that. Think about what I've been going through all week, working every night, trying to get through a lousy perform-ance in a play in front of hundreds of people, knowing all the time that Gloria is dying. I'm tired, I'm upset. I'm in a state of shock.'

'You'll be in an even worse state of shock by the time I've finished with you.'

'Oh calm down,' I said. 'The doctor's in the house.'

'Well that's good. You'll be needing a fucking doctor in the house if I lay my hands on you!'

'Stop it!' Jessie pleaded and pointed to the room above. 'The two of you, please, stop it. Everybody's in a terrible mood. This business has got to everybody.'

Joe and I stopped shouting and stood silently facing each other.

The kettle came to the boil and, as if announcing the 'all clear', slowly whistled away.

'Just make a cup of tea for yourselves,' I said. 'I think I'll go out for a while.'

While Joe still had his teeth clenched, I thought it the perfect time to go looking for hotel rooms for Tim and Paulette. So I grabbed my coat and left the house.

As I reached the end of the road I could see my brother's abandoned car. I hurried by, cursing it, then turned the corner into Aigburth Drive and headed for the park.

All my memories of Sefton Park are of hot summer Sundays and women in pretty frocks. I would often spend time there as a child, either being taken by my sister Mary and her husband or following after John and Frank and their gang. Some days we would take a boat out on the lake, or I would play around the dome-shaped glass house which harboured exotic plants and enormous palm trees which I was certain came from Africa. At times a travelling funfair would arrive, or maybe a circus, and set itself up on the north playing-fields, along by the avenue of trees.

I walked up the avenue, across the playing fields, past the glass house towards the hotels on the other side of the park.

The first hotel was full. There was a conference taking place and they had been booked up for months; however, if I were to telephone the next day there might be a cancellation. At the second hotel I was able to make a provisional booking for two single rooms.

It stopped raining on the way home. By the time I reached the end of our road the sun was almost out. As I turned the corner my mother and Jessie were just walking past Joe's car.

'We're just venturing out to the shops while the rain holds off,' my mother smiled reassuringly. 'I'm worried about you. You'd better get back to the house and dry yourself off.'

'Where's Joe?' I asked.

'He's upstairs with Gloria, so don't mention anything to him,' Jessie said cautiously. 'You know what he's like. He's been working all night. Anyway, he'll be all right once he's had something to eat.'

'Oh, I don't know what to buy for the easiest. If the chip shop's open we'll bring some back.' Then in a hushed voice, almost like a conspirator, my mother added, 'I'll get you a nice fish.'

Gloria looked at me, smiled and closed her eyes. Joe didn't speak and neither did I. When I sat on the side of the bed next to her she opened her eyes again.

'Sit me up, Peter,' she said.

I helped her to a sitting position, sideways on the bed with her feet on the floor.

'Burp me, Peter,' she whispered.

I started to rub her back. Without hesitation, Joe came and sat behind her, lending her support with his body. He and I still hadn't said a word to each other, but as my hand rubbed between their backs, not only was I burping Gloria, I was also burping Joe. It was difficult not to find the situation comic. He turned to me and smiled, and the tension between us relaxed. Joe and I were friends again, and Gloria became more alert.

'That feels so good,' she said. 'How am I doing, Joe?'

'You're doing great,' he replied. 'Just you carry on.'

She clicked her tongue against the roof of her mouth, pushed her fist ahead of her and put her thumb up, just like a champion, as she always did when things were going well.

Joe left the room. I helped Gloria back into her bed.

'There's a fish for Joe and a fish for you,' my mother said as I sat down at the kitchen table. 'Jessie, you asked for the fish cake. I'm just going to fry meself an egg because I didn't fancy any of that grease. The Chinese chip shop was shut, so we had to go to the Greek.'

'Oooh, their chips are lovely.'

'Well, Jessie, you just take more for yourself. I only want a few on a butty.'

'Oh no. I don't want any more. Give them to Joe.'

Joe put his paper down to look over his mountain of chips.

'Hang on, give some of them to our Peter. He looks as if he needs a good scoff.' Then he turned to me. 'How was Gloria when you left her?'

'She's resting now, but I think she's feeling a little bit better.'

'Well I think she's marvellous. A real fighter, that woman. She's got guts. I suppose that's what helped to make her a big star.'

'That's what the doctor said to me this morning,' my mother shouted over from the frying pan. 'He said that he couldn't believe the determination she's got.'

'She's certainly determined,' Joe said. 'She was almost cracking jokes when I was with her.'

'She's asked me to clean her nails,' I told them. 'But they look as if they've been done.'

'They have,' my mother said and joined us at the table. 'I did them this morning.' Then she added in a whisper, 'The doctor said she'll be doing this a lot now. Rambling and getting obsessed with things. He said there's nothing any of us can do for her except try to keep her as comfortable as we can.'

We all fell silent again.

'Does he think she might be in any pain?' Jessie eventually asked.

'Well love, he says that now she might be. I think he'd like to give her something but she still won't let him attend to her properly. Anyway, I had a good talk to that doctor this morning and he agrees with me that we should get a nurse to come into the house. Now I know that you'll say that she doesn't want one, Peter, but she's got to have the necessary attention. She needs bed baths and things, she could get sores. I know that Gloria doesn't want a nurse but she's not responsible for herself now.'

I had to agree, we all agreed. Gloria must have a nurse.

'We'll have to go "private". Gloria's American,' Jessie said. 'We'll never get one on the National Health.'

'Well, where are we going to get one from?'

It was at this point that I thought about Barbara at the vasectomy clinic.

The play I was in had a serious theme wrapped up in a comic structure and was set in a vasectomy clinic. During rehearsals it was thought a good idea that I went along to a clinic to talk to the staff and find out how vasectomies were performed. On the day of my visit, which I wasn't looking forward to, I was met by a strange-looking woman of uncertain age, with dangling arms, stretched see-through skin, apricot-coloured hair and wearing a grey uniform that was heavily starched. She looked like an X-ray dressed up.

'I'm Barbara Brawnsley. I'm the Duty Staff Nurse.' She then looked knowingly into my eyes and started to move her lips about, as if swilling something distasteful around the inside of her mouth. 'I hope you're not sensitive,' she quipped, then grabbed hold of my arm and led me into the building.

Up two flights of stairs and at the end of a corridor, we arrived at the door to an office. She sat down and picked up a cigarette that had been burning away in an ashtray on the desk in front of her. She inhaled deeply, then held her breath as the upper part of her body went into mild convulsions while she held back the coughs.

'Don't worry about me,' she said. 'It's only a tickle.'

I sat down at the other side of the desk.

'Now I've spoken to the director,' she went on, 'and he's told me all about it and what he wants. I'm sending over a trolley and some instruments to the Playhouse tomorrow. I haven't got much time so what I'm going to do is go through the procedure for a vas. You're going to watch and I'll pretend to be the patient. We've got to hurry up because the nurses are setting things up now. If you want a cigarette you can smoke in here, but nowhere else, and I'll have to ask you to wear these plastic bags on your feet.'

She handed me a pair of cellophane-looking boots and took me into the operating theatre to meet her nursing staff. They were young, lively and chatty, but Barbara bossed them about a lot and complained out loud about them to me. However, her way of doing it was very light-hearted and affectionate and the girls responded by laughing at her and pulling faces behind her back.

The afternoon went well. When it came to watching a real vasectomy operation, dressed up as a doctor, it wasn't as bad as I had anticipated.

Barbara and her girls were helpful and enthusiastic, but Barbara enthused the most. As rehearsals went on she would often come to the theatre, or telephone, to ask how things were going and to offer her advice, wanting to take on a responsibility for the production that was unnecessary but endearing. All the actors and stage staff became fond of her, and she booked tickets for a party of twenty people on the opening night of the play. Barbara loved the theatre.

'I've got an idea,' I said to the family. 'Barbara Brawnsley.'

'Who's Barbara Brawnsley?' my mother asked.

'She's a nurse and she works at the vasectomy clinic. She'll be able to help us out.'

'Oh Peter, are you sure?'

'Yes, it's all right, Jessie. Everything's going to be fine. I'll go and telephone her now.'

'Tell her to leave her scissors behind,' Joe shouted after me. 'I've got plans for the future.'

Dressed in an old gabardine raincoat, and a plastic headscarf covering her strange orange hair, Barbara arrived at the house twenty-five minutes later.

I took her straight to the kitchen to meet the family, who, after the initial shock, seemed just as taken with her as

I was. She quickly made herself at home, sitting around the kitchen table chattering and drinking cups of tea.

After being given a brief summary of the situation, Barbara was very practical and professional, drawing up a comprehensive list of things that might be needed, which included items such as bedlinen, plastic undersheets, antiseptics, swabs and the necessary things that would make it easier to give Gloria bed baths.

'Oh Nurse, it's marvellous that you could come.' My mother poured another cup of tea as Barbara lit her fourth cigarette. 'All my nerves have gone and I've been in a terrible state, especially as I'm going to Australia early next week.'

'Well, isn't it a small world?' Barbara exclaimed. 'I lived in Australia for over four years. I was a nurse in Alice Springs. You'll have a wonderful time, Australia's a very nice place.'

'Were you doing vasectomies over there?' Joe asked with a grin on his face.

'Oh no,' Barbara replied. 'I never touched a vas till I was over fifty, but I've done most everything else.'

My mother was reassured; Jessie was fascinated; and Joe was completely amazed.

'Well, let me go and have a look at her,' she said. 'I must see what has to be done.'

'The thing is, Barbara, Gloria doesn't like nurses and has said that she doesn't want one in the house. We have to be very delicate, I don't want her to get frightened.'

'That's not a problem, Peter,' she said between coughs. 'Who'd ever think that I was a nurse? If it wasn't for my qualifications I could easily be the patient.'

*

'What's that, Peter?' Gloria focused on Barbara, sitting in the corner of the room.

'That's Barbara,' I said.

'Well tell her to go away.'

'She's come to help.'

'I don't want her help. Tell her to go away.'

Without saying anything, Barbara stood up and left the room. I followed out after her and joined her on the stairs.

'I'm sorry, Barbara, but I did tell you it would be a bit difficult.'

'Don't worry, she'll get used to me. As soon as I've given her a good bed bath and a back support she'll feel much more comfortable.'

Barbara set to work immediately when we were back in the kitchen. She wanted to know what my mother had available in the house, and added some things to her list.

'Now, it just so happens that I've got the weekend off from the clinic, so if you like I can be here most of the time.'

'Oh, Nurse, that would be lovely.' My mother's face relaxed into a look of welcome relief. 'It would be really lovely.'

'Oh, I'm looking forward to it,' Barbara beamed. 'I've never had a film star through my hands before.'

I sat next to Gloria on her bed. She had a vacant look on her face.

'Do you want me to fix your pillow?' I said. 'Do you want me to shade the lamp?'

Gloria didn't respond.

I took hold of her left hand and began to clean her nails,

but she had no idea what I was doing, so I stopped before I reached the thumb.

It was nearly time for me to leave for the theatre, so I closed the curtains and left the room.

'That nurse has gone to the clinic to collect all the things on her list, but she's coming back later,' my mother said when I went to get my coat from the kitchen. 'She's a bit strange to look at but she seems to know what she's doing. I think she's a very nice woman.'

Knowing that Barbara liked gin, I quickly went out and bought a bottle before I left for the theatre so that she could fix herself a drink when she got back to the house. I was grateful she had come to help at such short notice.

The bus was empty except for a fidgety old man sitting on the seat nearest the driver, the one reserved for the aged. His body arched forward while his hands separated his knees. He wore a cap pulled over to one side and his shoes were newly Cherry Blossomed. Two seats in front of me sat a lonely woman holding a sleeping child.

I was sitting on the long seat at the back, looking out at the people queuing in the chip shops and going to the pubs. It was a Friday night and there was money to spend.

The bus pulled up at every stop along Aigburth Road, although nobody got on until we reached the Dingle, where a group of women were waiting outside the Bingo.

'Any luck tonight, girls?'

'Well if there was, love, we wouldn't be on your bus. We'd have been home long ago in a taxi.'

They all started to laugh as they paid their fares.

I got off the bus at Blackler's and walked through the precinct to Williamson Square.

The theatre was deserted. Not even the old girl who sold the programmes and the chocolates had set up her kiosk in the foyer. There was no sign of Old Jack – he was probably in the pub – and there was no one in the Green Room. I bought myself a cup of coffee from the machine and took it up to the third floor. The corridor was in darkness. I thought it strange that no one had been round to turn on the lights, but when I reached my dressing room the door was open, and Gil was sitting inside.

'I was just writing you a note,' she said.

'Where is everybody? The place is empty.'

'You're in a daze. We don't start till eight tonight. Anyway, sit down. I want to find out what's the matter with you.'

The Friday night audience was particularly appreciative and the evening passed by very quickly. Gil was waiting for me at the stage door and insisted on driving me home.

I was tired, but at least it was comforting to know that Barbara was now in the house looking after Gloria. I felt certain that her presence and professional status would bring a degree of order and stability.

I was wrong.

'Peter. We can't get that nurse out of the house.' My mother and father met me at the door. 'She won't go home and she's drunk.'

'What do you mean, she's drunk?'

'Why did you give her that bottle of gin? She's nearly

finished the lot!' My mother was almost hysterical. 'I thought she was giving Gloria a bed bath but when I went up to the room I found poor Gloria lying on one bed and that woman on the other with the bottle.'

Just then Barbara staggered into the hall.

'What's been going on?' I asked her. 'What's happened to Gloria?'

'She's a very difficult woman, Peter. She won't let me do a thing for her. She's definitely gone funny in the head. They all do that near the end. What she needs is Miss Euphoria.'

'What's Miss Euphoria?'

'It's a cocktail of morphine and gin. She wouldn't know what was happening to her. It's very nice.'

'Call Barbara a taxi,' I said to my mother and ran up the stairs to Gloria's room.

'I don't want that woman in here. Get rid of her, Peter.' Gloria was sitting up, leaning against the bed support, looking frightened and furious.

Suddenly Barbara burst into the room.

'See what I told you? What she needs is Miss Euphoria.'

I grabbed Barbara's arm and led her out of the house.

'She was being wonderful until she opened that bottle,' my mother said at the door. 'I suppose that's what comes from having a nurse who works at a vasectomy clinic.'

'I don't know about Gloria being the one who can't say "No",' my father added. 'It's that nurse who can't say "No". Especially when it comes to the gin.'

SIX

When I woke up in the room, she was sleeping. She was breathing; that's how I knew she was sleeping.

She couldn't speak much, but there was no need for talk. Sometimes she wanted the window to be shut, later she wanted it to be opened again. It didn't take long for us to fall into a routine; we knew each other well.

It had been a cold night outside, and with the wind and the rain coming in through the window, just as cold inside. The cold air was helping her to breathe, and as long as she was able to breathe, she was alive.

It was dark. It was early. It was a dark, early morning. I knew it was morning when a light was switched on in a house somewhere opposite; the man there delivered the news.

'She's getting worse.'

'I know.' My mother nodded her head and reached for a cup and a mug.

It was unusual to see her wearing her nightgown, but it was only just daylight; too early to be dressed and up out of bed. No one had slept well.

'This whole situation is getting worse. I don't think I can take any more.' She sat down to pour the tea. 'I've never known anything like it. I'll be glad when that son and the daughter arrive.'

'Gloria still doesn't know anything about them coming.'

'Well, let's just pray that she has time to find out. Only I hope they're not drug addicts or loonies. I couldn't go through another session like the one I had with that nurse.'

'When did you find Barbara was drinking?'

'I didn't even know that she'd started. She was very busy and being marvellous up until about half past nine. Then she came down here to the kitchen holding a thermometer, but waving it about like a wand. "Do you know what?" she said. "The beautiful actress has just told me that I'm something very rude." Then she disappeared back up to the room in a huff. Well, I thought, if she's a nurse she must be used to insults, and if she's worked in Australia she's bound to know what life's about. Then half an hour later I started to wonder. That's when I went up to the bedroom and found her with the gin. It seems that the one minute she was sober and the next minute she was drunk.'

For the rest of the morning the house was alive with activity; it pulsated with a feeling of urgency, while Gloria was getting weaker, worsening by the hour.

My mother was in a frenzy throughout but battled on with the housework, cleaning the hall, the front steps, the floor in the kitchen; the curtains in the living room were only halfway pulled back. It was as if she was getting prepared.

My father and Candy, who had been continually shunted from one room to another, accused of getting in the way, ended up down in the stores.

Jessie arrived early, but alone; Joe had another problem with his car.

'The battery was going flat, so he's gone to the garage to have it recharged. Otherwise it would have been dead by the end of the day.'

'Well it's a good thing he's not here,' my mother stated. 'He'd go mad if he heard what happened with that Barbara.'

Jessie took over the nursing.

There was a never ending stream of telephone calls and many to be made. Friends of mine, friends of Gloria's, her agent, were now all concerned. The director and staff from the theatre in Lancaster, who had been telephoning every day, were brought up to date with the news.

Eileen Connolly phoned to ask if she should come over, my sister Mary offered to help, and Barbara Brawnsley phoned to ask if she should come back.

'Only if I do,' she said, 'don't think of me as a nurse, but more as a friend of the family.'

My mother put her off.

The hotel into which I'd booked Tim and Paulette phoned to say that they'd have to accept another booking unless the rooms could be secured. So they were cancelled; we still didn't know when they would arrive.

Gloria's former husband, Tony Ray, phoned several times from New York. He was upset and very emotional. He said that he'd try and come to England, but he was told that he'd probably be too late.

My own sadness was distracted by the events of the day and the things that had to be done, but it was impossible to stop thoughts and pictures of Gloria from flooding my mind. Everyone was talking about her.

'Peter –' my mother was wiping over the table with the dish cloth – 'do you remember the time me and Jessie took her down to Great Homer Street market when she wanted to buy a pair of second-hand shoes? Ahhh, poor Gloria, it must be terrible to have her problem with those awkward feet. Of course it was early, there was no point in getting there late. But when we got there it was chocka. You had to keep tight hold of your purse. Thank God nobody cottoned on to who she was. Gloria just blended in with the crowds. She never ever tried to show herself off. She just went round all the stalls looking for her own few little bits. We had a great laugh with her that day. I wish we were doing that now.'

It was Saturday. There was a matinée. I'd put off leaving for the theatre as long as I possibly could; I was hoping to hear from Paulette and Tim. There was the possibility that their flight was late, or they'd missed it, or even, at the last minute, decided not to come. It was unbearable waiting for news, so I dialled Paulette's number in California several times, only to hear that slow infuriating tone, which hopefully confirmed that they were on their way.

I was late again for the half-hour call before the beginning of the play.

'You've been pushing it all week. This has got to stop.' Old Jack followed me halfway up the stairs to the dressing rooms, issuing threats.

Geoffrey, with his make-up on, was standing out in the corridor in a fit of pique.

'Actors being late. It puts everyone into a state of nervous tension. This is a theatre, not a come as you please.'

Ten minutes later I took my place alongside Gil in the wings. She gave me her usual wink before I walked onto the stage to deliver the opening line of the play.

The matinée was slow. It was dull. The small audience of elderly ladies who'd come out for their Saturday afternoon's entertainment were not impressed. There were no flowers at the curtain call.

I spent the gap between the matinée and the evening show, usually a time for rest, a time to recover from the first performance and build up energy for the second, waiting to speak on the telephone, to be brought up to date with what was happening at home. The one pay-phone backstage was in continual use, with actors making arrangements for Saturday night. While I waited, I had to listen to Geoffrey telling a story I'd heard a hundred times before. Linda was trying hard not to look unimpressed.

'It was during the banquet scene. Raymond was being marvellous, got slaughtered by the critics, but I thought he had a good stab. Anyway, I heard a very loud snore from the stalls, which persisted, and that's when Julia turned her gaze directly at me. She could be a prima-donna but she loved a bit of a joke, a bit of a comedienne she was really, not cut out for tragedy, poor love. All she had to do was raise an eyebrow, that's all she had to do to get a laugh, and that's exactly what she did. I went, she went, we all started to laugh; it was the most unforgettable corpse.'

When at last I dialled my parents' number, the line was continually engaged, driving me to the point of near despair;

I was anxious for any news about Gloria; I wanted to know if Paulette and Tim had arrived.

The evening show went well. The audience were demanding but out to enjoy themselves; they laughed at all the right lines.

'Great show tonight.'

'Isn't it going well?'

I couldn't share their enthusiasm. I couldn't wait for it to finish.

As soon as the play was over I asked Gil to give me a lift home.

'Well,' she gasped as she drew up outside the house. 'Good luck. I hope your visitors are here. If there's anything I can do . . .' She gave me a sympathetic smile as she drove off.

I stood on the pavement under the light from the lamp. The house gave nothing away; gave no clue as to who might be inside. Then I saw Joe's car, back from the garage, parked a few yards down the street. I opened the gate and walked up the path.

'They're here. They've arrived.'

As my father opened the front door wider I could see an array of baggage in the hall.

'I'll be glad to get away to Australia,' he said. 'There's too much going on for me here.' He walked down the passage towards Candy, who was waiting for him at the entrance to the stores.

'Sssh.' My mother put her finger to her lips. 'They're upstairs.'

Along with Joe and Jessie she was at the kitchen table.

There was an uneasy atmosphere about; strangers were in the house.

'What time did they get here?'

'Well,' Joe said in a whisper. 'The train was late for a start, but I had no trouble spotting them walking down the platform. It was the girl I saw first.'

'She's the spitting image of Gloria,' my mother announced, as if she was the first person to spot the resemblance. 'You can hardly tell them apart.'

'Yes, she does look like her in that film about the circus,' Jessie added. 'The one with Charlton Heston. It was on the telly just the other week.'

'Anyway,' Joe continued, 'I got them back here at about ten o'clock. We had a little talk, I filled them in with the details, told them what's been happening. Ever since, they've been upstairs with Gloria.'

'I've hardly seen them,' my mother declared. 'They wouldn't have anything to eat, not even a cup of tea. They brought their own food with them. It looks like seaweed but it's supposed to be a health drink.'

'Paulette looks upset. She's very pale.'

'Well, Jessie, naturally she would be. That only makes sense. But all the same, she could do with some decent food. Those Americans make themselves sick with all those vitamins.'

'I'll make a cup of tea.'

'That's a good idea, Jessie. That's my health drink.'

'What's Tim like?'

'Well he hasn't said a lot up to now, except that he wants to take a look at the situation. He wants to have a word with the doctor, think about things and then make quick decisions. He seems sensible enough but I don't know, Pete. I don't know anything about the lad.'

'I don't know much either, Joe. I've never met him before.'

Tim was Gloria's oldest child by her second husband, Nick Ray. Theirs was a complex relationship as Gloria's fourth husband, Tony, was also Tim's older half-brother; they both shared the same father. Gloria's fourth marriage therefore turned Tim's brother, Tony, into his step-father, and his mother into his sister-in-law.

Gloria told me that at one point Tim had worked in the film business. He'd recently travelled around India, but was now studying acupuncture.

I knew Paulette reasonably well, having spent some time with her on my visit to California. She used to come to the trailer quite a lot and we all went out to dinner a few times. She was a shy person and a bit nervous. She loved living near the ocean and wanted to work with animals. I liked her.

Just then she opened the kitchen door and hovered at the top of the stairs with a bowl in her hand. Wearing a thermal jacket over a heavy knit woollen sweater that reached her chin, she looked as if she was dressed for the Winter Olympics but somehow ended up in the wrong event.

'Excuse me, could I get some ice? I'd like to bathe Mom's face. And do you have an ice-crush?'

'Paulette.'

'Oh hi, Peter,' she said when she turned and saw me. 'How are you?'

'Okay. I'm sorry I wasn't here to meet you off the train.'

'Oh that's all right, Peter. When we called up from London, your mother said that you were at the theatre. That's fine.'

By this time my mother was fighting with the ice-cube tray, bashing it against the sink.

'Here you are, love. Come down and get it. It's in little bits and it'll look more crushed once it's started to melt. Oh,' she said, 'I hate these trays that stick to your fingers.'

I'm sure that the bashed-about ice-cubes were not quite what Paulette had in mind, but she smiled, expressed her gratitude and then went back up to her mother.

'I'd better go and say hello to Tim,' I said.

'Now hold on a minute.' My mother pulled a chair back for me at the table. 'Don't be in so much of a hurry.'

'Hi, I'm Tim.'

'I'm Peter. Hello.'

Tim stood in the doorway. I could hardly see into Gloria's room. Not much older than myself, he was about the same height and had short, dark, curly hair. He leant against the door-frame and spoke to me confidentially.

'I'll be coming to speak to you later, Peter, but right now I'm trying to talk to Mom. Communication is a problem but it's important to try and find out how she feels about things before I assess the situation and decide what's best to do.'

'That's fine, Tim,' I said. 'I just wanted to tell you that I had a problem finding a hotel, so it's a question of making do here tonight. My mother will talk to you about the sleeping arrangements before she goes to bed. At some point I want to come in and see Gloria, and I'd definitely like to have that talk.'

'Oh for sure, Peter. Of course. Let's talk later,' he said as he closed the door.

I went to the upstairs sitting room. I felt I needed to be alone.

'Christ, I'm exhausted,' Tim said as he flopped into the comfortable armchair.

'You must be,' I said. 'It's a long journey.'

'Especially after reaching London,' Tim replied. 'And it's so cold here. Is it always this cold? I can see why The Beatles left town.'

'Liverpool is like New York, Tim. It gets a lot of wind from the river.'

'It's freezing in Mom's room.'

'That's because she needs the window open most of the time. It's helping her to breathe.'

'But Peter, don't you think that it's freezing in here, too?'

'I'm sorry that you've had to come,' I said, changing the subject to the main purpose of the visit.

'Yeah, Peter. It's tough.'

'How is Gloria tonight?'

'Well, Peter, she's weak. She's not saying much so I'm trying to establish a positive method of communication. The weight loss is drastic. It's too bad that she hasn't had solid food.'

'Well, as you can see for yourself, Gloria is not able to take solid foods and she can hardly drink. We have tried to feed her but she is just too ill to take it.'

'I'd like to know the history of this illness.'

'Yes, so would I. It was only last Tuesday when I found out she was sick.'

Tim and I embarked on a question and answer session. He wanted to know all the details of Gloria's visit since she'd arrived from Lancaster. I told him everything I knew, pointing out the fact that Gloria had persistently refused medical attention and that I was advised by the health authorities that I could be committing an offence if I were to force her to have treatment that she did not want.

'Well, how come you have a doctor? I hear he's been around a few times. I gather Mom doesn't seem to like him too much.'

'The health authorities advised it. He's not able to treat Gloria against her wishes but the reason he is here is to monitor her illness and make sure that nothing strange has been happening.'

'Your brother told me that this afternoon the doctor was talking about a death certificate and of the possibility of having to fly the body back to America. How come it's so certain that she's dying?'

I went back to the beginning of the story, telling Tim about Gloria's collapsing during a rehearsal of the play up in Lancaster, about Joe and Jessie taking me up there and the telephone conversation I'd had with the doctor from the hospital.

'Doctor Casey has confirmed the situation and I'm afraid Gloria's death is very imminent.'

'I have to go to the bathroom,' Paulette said as she came into the room. She was almost in tears. 'Tim, will you sit with Mom?'

'I'd like to sit with her,' I said.

'That's okay, Peter. I'll take a look down in the kitchen and have a talk with your folks.'

I closed the door firmly behind me. I wanted to be alone with Gloria.

She looked different. Each time I saw her she looked different. It was her hair. Jessie and my mother would always try to make it look nice but they each had their own way of doing it, so it had been through a variety of styles; brushed back off her face, pulled across to the side, and fluffed up with strands combed into curls at the front. She looked at me, stone-faced and miserable. She didn't smile.

'Tim and Paulette.'

'Yes, I telephoned them.'

Gloria turned her head away and closed her eyes.

The door opened and Paulette came into the room.

'What are we going to do, Peter?' she whispered.

'I'm not sure, Pauli. Let's wait and see what Tim thinks.'

We sat in silence.

'I've never been in an aeroplane before,' my mother was telling Tim across the kitchen table.

'You're kidding,' he said, surprised. 'You're gonna love the experience.'

'Everyone says that it's a horrible noise.'

'Don't you believe it, you won't hear a thing. Just carry a Walkman.'

'Oh no,' my mother said. 'I've already got too much to carry about, and I've got to stop off in Manila.'

She had no idea what a Walkman was.

'Has everything been fixed up?' I said. 'Do Tim and Paulette know where they're sleeping?'

'Yes, Joe and Jessie have gone for tonight, so I've put them in the room they were in. They'll have to share it though, but it's the best I can do.'

'That's fine,' Tim said. 'We won't be sleeping tonight anyway, but if we do it will be on a rota basis.'

'Well, work it out amongst yourselves. I've got to get some sleep.' My mother wished us goodnight and then she went to bed. I was alone with Tim.

'Well, I'd like Mom to get some proper medical attention as soon as possible.'

'It may be that a private clinic is the answer.'

'Well, as I said, Peter—' Tim stood up from the table and spoke to me very earnestly – 'I will attempt to find out how Mom feels about it and I will also discuss it with Paulette. Maybe I'll call Joy in California. I'd also like to talk with that doctor of yours, but I'll be making a decision, probably during the next ten hours.'

Legally, being Gloria's eldest child, I supposed that he was the only person responsible for making a decision on her behalf, but as Gloria could barely speak I wondered how Tim was going to find out how she felt about the various possibilities.

'Tim,' I said, 'I hope that you don't think that I'm pushing you to make your decisions but I'm sure that you realize how ill Gloria is. I think if you can persuade her to go to a hospital, a hospice, anywhere, the sooner she gets the attention the better.'

'Well, Peter. I still have to think about the whole thing properly. Mom is a very strong-willed and determined lady.'

'I know that she's strong and I know that she's determined, but she is dying.' Tim had gone. I said the words out loud to myself.

The door to Gloria's room was closed. I felt completely at a loss. I couldn't make her get better again. I was in no position to make the decisions. This wasn't my house and Gloria was no longer my responsibility.

SEVEN

The church bells were ringing, a solemn and empty sound, announcing it was Sunday.

Tired and uncomfortable, I woke up on the couch in the upstairs flat.

'Get down those stairs! I thought I told you not to come up here, you bad dog. There'll be hairs all over everywhere.' My mother was disciplining Candy on the landing outside.

'What time is it, Mum?' I called.

'Just turned ten o'clock.' She put her head around the upstairs living room door.

'What's happened to Gloria?'

'Paulette's in with her now and her brother's talking on the phone, but I don't know who to. He's spoken to the doctor, who's coming here in less than half an hour, so I want to get this room tidied. They can talk in here. Do you think you'll get up?'

'Yes, Mum. I'm about to get up.'

In contrast to the defiant noise of the church bells and the cold of the upstairs flat, the kitchen was quiet and warm. There was a stack of clothes that had been ironed, sitting on the sideboard, and a delicious lingering smell of the hot iron and cotton that had been slightly singed.

Paulette looked tense and uncomfortable as she came down the few steps into the room.

'Oh hi, Peter,' she said when she saw that I was the only one there. 'Can I boil up some water?'

'Of course you can. Come and have some coffee.'

'Oh no thanks, Peter. I just want to fix the vitamin drink and take it up to Mom.'

'Has she been able to drink it?'

'Well no, but she's been trying. Is that the tea kettle?'

Paulette moved across the room, put water into the kettle and then put it on the gas. Although it wasn't cold in the kitchen, she stood over the kettle with her hands around the flame, waiting for it to boil.

'Are you cold, Paulette?'

'No, Peter. I don't know. I don't think so.'

'Would you like to have a bath?'

'Oh no, Peter. Thank you. I'm gonna have some sleep.'

'Didn't you sleep much during the night?'

'I tried but I couldn't.' Her voice suddenly broke. 'Why has she done this, Peter? Why has she let this happen?'

'I don't know, Paulette. You probably know much more than me.'

'When she was in California, Peter, she got very neurotic and bad-tempered and I guessed that something was wrong, but then she went away and acted in a play somewhere. When she got back she seemed okay, but then she got sick again and was very weak. So I fed her with broth, Peter, and good food and she slowly got better again. And she was sweet, she just wanted to be in the trailer. She seemed happy.

She did dishes and things, tended the garden and just wanted to be happy.'

'Paulette, why didn't you try to let me know what was happening?'

'Mom didn't want you to know, Peter. She didn't want anybody to know. I guess she didn't wanna upset people.'

'Well, how about her sister? Did Joy know Gloria was sick?'

'She sort of knew, but it was difficult because Mom would never tell anybody anything. Then she seemed to get better and wanted to come to England to work on the play. I didn't want her to come, nobody did, but I didn't think this would happen.'

'But Paulette, why didn't you get any proper help? Why didn't she see a doctor?'

'You know, Peter, I think Joy had the same kind of thing a long time ago, but she had surgery and now she's fine. And Grandma, she had surgery because she had something wrong too, and now she's an old lady. Mom just doesn't like doctors.'

The water came to the boil. The church bells started to ring again. The light coming in through the window dulled and the rain clouds were gathering. It was letting out time at the church and anyone who had gone there was likely to get wet.

'The doctor's about to arrive,' my mother announced at the kitchen door. She was wearing her Sunday morning outfit – the cooking and cleaning mix-and-match – an apron and a headscarf, tied behind the ears and tucked under at the back. 'I've just seen him pull up in a car while I was at the window straightening the folds in the curtains. He's stopped to say hello to the woman from number fifteen, the one who goes to church. She's got a face like a bacon butty. I wonder how he knows her?'

'What shall I do, Peter? What shall I do with this vitamin drink?'

'Look, Paulette love,' my mother came into the middle of the room. 'You'd better go and try to get your brother off the telephone. Will you tell him that the doctor's here? Then I'd go back to your mother. You might be able to persuade her to let the doctor do something for her.'

Paulette rushed up the stairs when the doorbell rang.

My mother went to the door.

'Oh, Doctor Casey. You look as though you've been standing about in the rain. Gloria's children have arrived.'

'Yes, yes. I did speak to the chappie on the telephone,' I heard the doctor reply.

'He doesn't seem too happy, that doctor,' my mother said as she came back into the room. 'I think he's a bit tired of coming here, especially as there's nothing for him to do.'

'I think Tim will be able to persuade Gloria to go to a hospital.'

'Well if he does,' my mother answered, 'it won't be a hospital in Liverpool. He's talking about taking her back to America.'

'You must have got it wrong. That would be impossible.'

'I would have thought so.' My mother closed the kitchen door and sat down at the table. 'I was just running over the banister with a duster,' she said, 'just at the top of the stairs, right outside the room where Tim was talking on the phone.

I heard him say, to whoever it was, I don't know who it was, that he was thinking of taking his mother back to America.'

'Gloria's dying!'

'Well, I'm just telling you what I heard him say. I might have got it wrong, but I don't think that I have because I also heard him say that he's discussed it with her and that she says that she wants to go.'

'Gloria can't speak,' I shouted, 'let alone discuss anything! Tim's crazy if he thinks he's taking Gloria back to America. He can't. I'm going to tell him that he can't!'

'Now stop it. Just stop it. Don't you get yourself worked up. No, it doesn't make any sense to me either. I think that it's the most stupid thing that I've ever heard, but it's nothing to do with us. Tim is Gloria's son and if he wants to take his mother, dying as she is, back to America on an aeroplane, then it's his decision and you, or anybody else, can't stop him. Maybe Gloria does want to go back. Maybe the family want their mother home with them in America. You just don't know what the situation is. Tim and Paulette have been up there with her all through the night, so they must be able to see for themselves what kind of condition she's in. Maybe they think it's best to take her back now, rather than later, if you know what I mean. You just don't know, so don't you interfere. Just keep out of it. To tell you the truth I'll be amazed if she's allowed to travel on a plane, the way she is. What she needs is an ambulance to take her to the nearest hospital, and if I had my way, she would have been in one days ago!'

I couldn't sit around wondering what was going on up-stairs, waiting to be told what was happening. I felt restless, annoyed, unprepared for another day of this endless confusion.

To the disapproval of my mother, who told me I was interfering, I rushed out from the kitchen and ran up to Gloria's room. Halfway up the stairs I stopped; I had to change my pace. There was a hollow, empty sensation in the pit of my stomach and suddenly I felt sick.

It was Sunday: inescapable, miserable Sunday. Suddenly quiet; suddenly still. What if we were all to be trapped here forever, I thought. This unlikely collection of people: a dying film star, her son who was also her brother-in-law, a doctor who was unable to do anything to help, two old age pensioners desperately trying to get to Australia, and a drunken nurse. All going crazy to the music of *The Pirates of Penzance*. It would soon become a living hell.

Gloria was alone.

She still looked like Gloria, only smaller, iller and grey. I sensed she didn't want me there. Was she hating me for the things I'd done? I'd left her alone for a night, I'd tried to persuade her to go to a hospital, I'd called a doctor, I'd found a drunken nurse, and I'd engineered the arrival of Tim and Paulette. I'd done everything she'd asked me not to do.

'Do you want to go back to America?' I could hear the panic and urgency in my voice.

She slowly shook her head from side to side.

'Do you want to go to the hospital here?'

She shook her head again.

'Well, Gloria, what do you want to do?'

I could see the confusion in her eyes. She had no idea

what was going on. It was cruel of me to ask her all these questions. I sat down on the bed and held her.

'Hello, Peter. Hello, Gloria.' Jessie came into the room. 'We've not long been here,' she whispered. 'Joe was wondering where you were, Peter. He's talking to Tim upstairs. Now that the doctor's gone, I thought I'd come and ask Gloria if she'd like to freshen up. I've brought her a little present. It's a headscarf, pink and pale green.'

'You're going to make yourself ill,' my mother called from the bottom of the stairs. 'I thought that I told you not to interfere. You'll only be thought badly of in the end. Take my advice and keep out of the way. You look shocking.' Then as a kind of warning she added, 'Your father's back.'

'What difference is that supposed to make?' I shouted at her.

She went away without saying another word and I knew that I had hurt her feelings.

Depressed, I walked on up the next flight of stairs towards the voices. Joe and Tim were talking. As I passed the bedroom I could hear Paulette weeping.

'What do you think we should do, Peter?' she asked when I sat next to her. 'Do you think we should take her back home?'

'I think she should go to the hospital in Liverpool.'

'Do you think the hospital will be able to save her?'

'Let's go and find out from Tim what the doctor had to say.'

'Have you been crying, Pauli?'

'I'm confused. I just don't know, Tim. Maybe we should

just take Mom to the hospital here in Liverpool. I just don't like to see her this way and maybe she just wouldn't make it back home. What do you think, Peter?'

'I think Gloria should stay in Liverpool.'

'But Peter –' Tim looked at Joe as he spoke to me – 'you know Mom won't go to a hospital here. I've talked to Mom and spoken to Joy, and I've found out that there's a doctor in New York that Mom trusts. I've persuaded her to let him take a look at her. She will make it back. She's a determined lady and I think that if going back to New York is the only chance we have for her, then we should take it.'

'Now look, Peter,' Joe spoke firmly. 'You know what all the problems are and what they have been over the last week. We've been unable to do anything or make any decisions for Gloria. Tim and Paulette have come here because they're the only ones who can make those decisions, and so I think that it should be left to them.' Then he turned to Tim. 'It's a decision for you and Paulette, and it's a difficult one. It might be the most difficult decision that you'll ever have to make. It's your mother. You'll never have to make a decision like it again.' He paused, then added, 'I think you want to take her home.'

'If it's the only chance, Joe, then yes, I think I do want to take my mother back home. Paulette, do you agree with me?'

'Okay, if it's going to help Mom.'

'Right.' Joe stood up. 'That's it. Let's get everything organized.'

'Let's go back to Mom, Pauli, and tell her what is going to happen. Right now she needs all the encouragement we can give. Thanks, Joe,' Tim said as he left the room. 'Thanks for what you had to say.'

'It's probably for the best, Peter,' Joe said when we were alone.

'Yes,' I replied. 'It's probably all for the best. But if I thought that Gloria could get better I'd be happy that she was going back, but she's not going to get better, is she? And so I'm not very happy.'

My mother came into the room and sat on the arm of the chair.

'Gloria's going back to America,' I said.

'Yes, I know,' she said. 'Tim's just told me. It's probably all for the best.'

'That's what we've just been saying, Mum. That it's probably all for the best.'

Joe and my mum nodded their heads at each other but for me, I wasn't convinced.

'Well,' my mother said after a while. 'We can eat soon, everything's nearly ready.'

'I'm hungry.' Joe gave her a hearty smile.

'Let's try to get back to normal now that we know what's going to happen. Let's all get back to the kitchen. Your father's downstairs. He's got the Sunday papers.'

My father stood in front of the gas fire, wearing his new cap. He had a carrier bag squashed into a pocket of his crumpled jacket and his baggy trousers hung loosely around his body, even though they were held up by a pair of braces and a leather belt.

'Papers, newspapers there.' He pointed over to a chair.

Joe sat down to read the *Sunday People* and I looked through a magazine. Jessie took more ice-cubes up to Gloria, and came down with dirty linen to be washed. My mother wondered if Tim and Paulette would like to eat, so Jessie went back up to the room to ask. She returned to say they didn't want anything at all. The food was served; we all sat in silence while we ate.

Throughout the meal I could hear the telephone 'ding', the noise it makes every time the receiver is picked up or put back down. Tim would be making calls, making the arrangements for Gloria to leave.

Paulette came down to the kitchen twice while we were eating; the first time to return the ice bowl, the second to boil up some water.

Towards the end of the meal, Tim put his head round the kitchen door to ask if he could have a private word with Joe, who then left the table to go away and talk. Jessie helped to clear away the plates and then went back up to Gloria's room. My mother washed the dishes. My father went to the stores. There seemed nothing for me to do.

'I'm going to drive Tim over to see the doctor.' Joe returned to the kitchen wearing his coat.

'Why, what's wrong?' my mother shouted from the sink.

'Nothing. We're going over to collect a note from him to say that Gloria has to be allowed to travel on the aeroplane to get back to New York for urgent medical treatment. Tim doesn't want a problem at the airport.'

'What else has Tim arranged?' I asked.

Joe sat down and told us that the flight had been booked; they would be travelling to London on the 6.20 from Liverpool airport the following morning. Then they would be taking a connecting flight from Heathrow to New York where an ambulance would be waiting to meet them.

'Well,' my mother wiped her hands on the tea towel. 'I'm amazed that it's all happening so quickly. I'm surprised the doctor's allowing her to go. They're taking a terrible risk.'

It was time, I thought, for me to take Candy for a walk.

The park was almost empty. A few kids were playing on the trunks of the fallen trees and a teenage courting couple were sitting on a bench outside the café, which was closed. Candy, obviously happy to be out of the house, ran on ahead, past the bandstand, along towards the slope that leads down to the lake. Then she stopped and waited for me to catch up.

Halfway along the path around the side of the lake, two figures in anoraks were huddled together, sitting on boxes and holding on to fishing lines. What a ridiculous thing to be doing, I thought, on a cold, wet and unpleasant Sunday afternoon. They didn't turn round as I walked towards them. They didn't even notice Candy. They had vacant, expressionless looks on their faces. Maybe they were like me, I thought, just wanting to keep out of their house and content to be killing time. I walked on to Old Nick's Cave.

When Candy was exhausted, I sat down on a bench and looked out across the lake. I knew it was raining because I was wet, but I couldn't see the rain, only feel it on my face; it wasn't making ripples or patterns on the surface of the water. I sat there for a long while. Only when Candy became restless did I notice that the fishermen were gone. It was time to go home. The nights were drawing in and soon it would be dark.

*

'You've been a long time.' My mother was down in the kitchen. 'I've made pies.'

'I can't see Joe's car. Is he still out with Tim?'

'No, they've been back for hours. Everything's been fixed up. Now Joe's gone to one of his jobs, but he's coming back later. Him and Jessie are staying the night, seeing how it's the last before Gloria goes.'

'Where's Jessie?'

'She's having a talk with Paulette.'

I sat on a chair in the corner, waiting, thinking, waiting for the end of the day.

'She's not very good at all,' Jessie announced at about nine-thirty. 'I just hope she doesn't get any worse before she has to go. No decision can be a good one. Can it, Peter?'

'No, not really,' I said.

'Are you going up to sit with Gloria at all?'

'No, not yet.'

My mother carried on with her ironing; Jessie thumbed through the magazines. I didn't speak. Nobody said anything. Not until Joe came home, which was after eleven.

'How is everything upstairs,' he asked.

'Gloria's not good,' Jessie answered. Then she started to cry.

'That will have to stop. You'll put everybody into a terrible state if you start all of that now.'

'Well, Joe. I'm worried about her.'

'And I'm worried too.' My mother put down the iron. 'What's going to happen? I mean what's going to happen in the morning? Nobody's told us anything.'

Just then Tim came into the kitchen.

'Pauli and I have come up with an idea, so I've come to put it to you folks.'

'What's that, love?' My mother folded a towel.

'Well, Pauli and I thought that the most sensible thing for us to do is to grab some sleep. We've got this whole travel operation to handle in the morning. And so I was wondering if anyone else could sit with Mom?'

'I'll be staying up tonight,' Joe said.

'And so will I,' added Jessie. 'I'll be with her.'

'Oh well, that will be perfect, if it's no bother. I've arranged for a taxi to pick us up at five-fifteen to take us to the airport. The other thing I wanted to ask is if there's any possibility of having a wake-up call at approximately four-thirty?'

'Well, you can have an alarm clock. But, as I said Tim, I'll be staying up tonight.'

'Okay, Joe. That's perfect, Peter, will you be around in the morning?'

'Yes, Tim. I'll be around.'

'Okay. Thank you everybody for all that's been done. I'm going to get some sleep.' He left the kitchen and went on up to bed.

'Well, I'm ready for the pillow myself. It's nearly midnight. Ah, look at these.' My mother picked up the last things to be ironed. 'It's Gloria's white blouse and her silk pyjamas. Poor Gloria.'

'Well, give them to me,' Jessie said after a short silence. 'I'll pack them in her suitcase. I'm going up now to sit with her through the night.'

'No, Jessie, Don't. Don't go.'

'But Peter, Gloria's by . . .'

'No, Jessie. Don't. I'm going to stay with her tonight.'

Jessie looked towards Joe, then my mother, before handing me the clothes.

'Okay, Peter. Okay, you go. If you want anything just come and tell me, Joe and I will be sitting down here in the kitchen.'

'You look very tired, Paulette.' She was standing at the top of the stairs, outside the bedroom door, 'Why don't you go to bed?'

'I don't like to leave her, Peter. Do you think that I should sit up through the night?'

'No, I'm going to be with her. I'll wake you, Paulette. Goodnight.'

'Okay, Peter. Goodnight.'

Gloria was oblivious to my presence.

The change in her was phenomenal. Her body looked smaller, her long slender legs shorter. Her skin turned a ghostly grey.

She lay breathing heavily, noisily. Her mouth was open wide. At times she would be quiet. Often for quite a while. Then the heavy, noisy breathing would start again and her head would droop to her chest, when she'd gasp and open her eyes.

I wiped her mouth and bathed her face with a damp sponge, but when she raised her hand, as if to say, 'That's enough', I left her side and sat in the armchair opposite.

Sometimes I thought she might recognize me. I thought she was trying to speak, but then her eyes would close, her head would go back onto the pillow and she was quiet until the heavy breathing started again. She was like that all through the night. I stayed there watching, sitting in the chair.

'Peter, it's nearly four,' Jessie whispered from the doorway. 'I've just made a pot of tea. Do you want me to take over for the last half hour?'

'No thanks, Jessie. I'll stay.'

'Okay, but I'll be back up very soon.'

Suddenly Gloria was breathing violently. She was moaning, she was groaning, she was gasping.

'Die. Gloria, die. Please die now. Don't fight any more. It's over for you, my darling. I'm sorry, but please don't go on with this. Die. Please die.'

She moaned. The light from the lamp flickered. For a second I wanted to put it out.

She fell silent.

'Gloria.'

We both gasped for air at the same time, and Gloria opened her eyes.

'Do you know what, Gloria?' Joe sat at the foot of the bed. 'You are a very remarkable woman.'

The room was suddenly crowded. Tim and Paulette arrived, dressed and ready to leave. My mother and Jessie appeared with hot tea.

'Okay,' Tim announced. 'What we need to do is get Mom ready to leave. We have a schedule to keep.' He went and sat down next to Gloria and held her. 'Mom, I'm going to get you back home, and to the hospital and the doctor you trust. But what you have to do to help me get you there is to give the greatest performance you've ever given. Is that a deal?'

Gloria nodded her head.

'Right, Pauli. Put the light on. Let's get going. She needs make-up.'

The overhead light was put on. Gloria moaned and closed her eyes; the light was very bright, she'd been in darkness for most of the week. There was an all-out burst of activity. Everything happened quickly. Paulette applied the make-up to Gloria's unresponsive face, just lipstick and eye shadow and a bit of colour on her cheeks. Jessie arranged her hair, the back of which was wrapped up in the headscarf, now made into a kind of snood. Tim packed the suitcase with Gloria's bits and pieces that had been lying about the room.

'What's she going to wear?' My mother panicked. 'She can't leave in that old nightdress.'

Jessie picked up the silk pyjamas. 'These, she can wear these.'

It was awkward getting Gloria into them because it was difficult for her to move her arms and legs. Gloria was frightened and confused and just wanted to be left sitting in the pyjamas on the edge of the bed.

Suddenly we heard loud knocking. It was the taxi to take her away. Now there was no turning back. Joe went down to open the door, then returned to take the suitcase and small black hold-all.

It was impossible for Gloria to step into her shoes, her only pair of shoes, the black suede stilettoes, the ones she liked so much. Instead she was put into a pair of thick woollen socks.

I quickly picked up the shoes and, before anyone noticed what had happened to them, I'd taken them to the bathroom and put them in a cupboard.

'I want to keep these shoes,' I thought.

The silk pyjamas were covered by her short, white fox-fur coat. Now she was ready to go, but it was impossible for Gloria to walk.

'Let's carry her down the stairs sitting on the chair,' someone suggested.

That's how she left the house.

I went down the stairs ahead to stop her falling. Joe and Tim carried her on the chair. Halfway down Gloria moaned and shook her head.

'I'll fall,' she whispered.

We stopped.

'No,' I said. 'She can't go.'

'Yes, she can, Peter. She must.'

The taxi man sounded his horn.

'Come on now. We're nearly there.'

Soon we were in the hallway. My mother kissed her on the cheek and then she was carried out.

Putting her into the taxi was difficult. Paulette sat inside with the bags, then we lowered the chair into a horizontal position, and she was passed into the back of the cab.

Tim sat next to his sister and held on to Gloria on the chair. It was unbearable and terrifying to see her sitting in the back of a taxi, on a dark, misty morning, on the small wooden chair.

The driver started the engine; slowly they moved away. Joe, Jessie and I followed behind in Joe's car.

It was fortunate that the taxi had arrived earlier than expected because the journey to the airport, which normally took fifteen minutes, took almost three quarters of an hour. Gloria couldn't travel very fast. The macabre procession travelled at a funereal pace. Sometimes Joe would overtake the taxi, or travel alongside it, so that we were able to look through the window, to see that everything was all right. Each time we passed the side of the taxi I would come face to face with the dreadful image of Gloria sitting on her chair, illuminated by the light inside the cab. I could have been watching rushes from a black and white silent film, with Gloria dressed in cream silk and white fox fur, the star – a tragic goddess from the silver screen.

Joe speeded ahead to the airport. We collected a wheel-chair and waited outside for Gloria to arrive. She got there with a few minutes to spare and was quickly transferred from one chair to the other and hurried to the departure gate.

The small airport was empty. The other travellers had boarded the flight; the plane was waiting for its last three passengers. It was strange that no questions were asked about Gloria, but a few of the airport workers gathered around, curious to find out why a woman in a wheelchair, dressed up in a glamorous fur coat, was leaving in such a hurry.

Suddenly it was time for her to leave. Joe and Jessie kissed her and then they moved away. I kissed her cheek and held her hand. She winked at me and smiled. We didn't say good-bye.

I watched her being wheeled away. I waited by the gate looking after her until she was out of sight.

Then somebody grabbed my arm: an airport worker, a

man in his forties. It took me a few seconds to work out what he was saying.

'Was that Gloria Grahame? Was that the film star?'

Later that day, a few hours after being admitted to St Vincent's Hospital, New York, Gloria died.

* * *

My mother and father did get to Australia.

Three days later I was at the same airport, at the same time. They were taking the same flight as Gloria had taken; the 6.20 a.m. to London's Heathrow.

My father, wearing his cap, was nervously pacing about, and my mother wearing her headscarf, but dolled up to the eyeballs, was giving me instructions as to how I was to look after the house.

'Make sure that Candy has water in her bowl on the floor by the kitchen sink, and remember that the milkman gets paid on a Saturday.'

I shook hands with my father and gave my mother a big kiss. Then I left them to board the flight which was to take them off on their long-awaited holiday.

As I walked away from the gate I was pulled by the shoulder, my arm was almost wrenched from my body. It was the same airport worker who had stopped me three days earlier to ask if Gloria was a film star.

'And who was that one?' he shouted. 'Tell me, who was she?'

I turned round and my mother was still waving at the

gate. 'It's another one,' he cried. 'I recognize the face. Tell me who she is.'

This time I smiled.

'That one,' I said, 'was Hedy Lamarr.'

Since Then

Reading my book thirty years after it was first published, what struck me most was how much more I know now about Gloria Grahame's achievements as an actress than I did then, and also how exciting it has been for me to see her stature grow. Yes, in the 1950s she did achieve Hollywood stardom, and indeed she does have her very own star cemented into Hollywood Boulevard (I've now seen it), but when we first met in the late 1970s she hadn't been in films for many years and so, in England, she wasn't generally known. If people did recognize her name it was only vaguely and there was a struggle to place her except as a B-movie actress who mostly played a floozy or a gangster's moll – 'Did her face get scarred by a pot of scalding coffee? 'Yes, that was in *The Big Heat* with Lee Marvin' – but that perception of her was wrong. It didn't quite sum her up.

Thirty years ago we didn't have DVDs, we didn't have the internet, film blogs, and we didn't have YouTube. Thanks to all that, I've now seen most of her films. When I first met her I couldn't tell her that I'd seen her in any; except the one about a train crash and a circus and an elephant, which was wedged somewhere in the back of my memory from a rainy Sunday afternoon watching the telly. Of course, now I know that film to be *The Greatest Show on Earth*, directed by Cecil B DeMille and which was nominated for five Oscars and won Best Picture. A wonderful film, and Gloria's performance in it playing Angel was stand-out. Her acting style was different, even alternative, and there was definitely something of the mystery about her. Looking at her performances, what sets her apart from most other actors on the screen is that she seems to be the only one who's thinking her character's private thoughts. She may be about to say something but, then thinking about it, she may change her mind and decide to say nothing. She'll just look, think, and leave us to figure her out. Francois Truffaut said of her that she was the only American actress who was a real person on the screen. The film critic Roger Ebert said that there was 'something fresh and modern about her', and in a 2015 article about her in the New York *Village Voice* to coincide with a retrospective of her films shown at the Lincoln Centre, Graham Fuller wrote that she 'was one of the greatest actresses of mid-twentieth-century Hollywood'.

Gloria worked for some of the great film directors like Edward Dmytryk, Vincent Minnelli, Frank Capra, Elia Kazan, Fritz Lang, and the impressive list goes on. She made over forty films including *It's a Wonderful Life* – in which she played Violet Bick; *Crossfire* – which she told me was her favourite and for which she was nominated for her first Academy Award; *A Woman's Secret*, *In a Lonely Place*, *Sudden Fear*, *The Bad and the Beautiful* – for which she won an Academy Award; *The Big Heat*, *Human Desire*, *Naked Alibi*, *The Cobweb*, *Not as a Stranger*, and *Oklahoma!* – which she told me she just hated because she couldn't sing, she couldn't dance, and she couldn't stand wearing 'that bonnet'. Gloria worked in films alongside some of Hollywood's legendary stars; Katherine Hepburn, James Stewart, Lucille Ball, Frank Sinatra, Humphrey Bogart, Charlton Heston, Lana Turner, Joan Crawford; and now, over a thirty-year timespan, I've witnessed her take her rightful place among them.

The passing of years has also given me more time to appreciate Gloria the woman herself rather than Gloria the film star, and to realize the privilege I was handed to have journeyed with her through several years of her life. Thinking back on the relationship we shared, I've laughed out loud at her knowing sense of humour and sighed at the memory of her blank and immovable stubbornness. And, oh yes indeed, I remember her irresistible vulnerability. But, above all, what has become so apparent to me now, which wasn't to me then, is how misunderstood Gloria was, and how brave she had been in dealing with the barrage of falsehoods and inaccuracies about her from her turbulent days in Hollywood, where she was the victim, certainly by today's standards, of psychological and physical abuse. No matter what had happened to Gloria in life, or would happen, she always found the courage to carry on.

Turning over the pages of my book has turned over memories and thoughts about Gloria which had been lying dormant for years; words, images, truths about her life and also my own, which can only be realized with time.

Gloria came to England in the spring of 1978 to play the role of Sadie Thompson in the Somerset Maugham play *Rain*, which was to have a three-week run at the Watford Palace Theatre just on the outskirts of London. It was fitting, and I was amused, that on the day she arrived she was greeted by a full-blown rain-bashed day. I wondered why this Oscar-winning actress I'd never heard of was not staying at the Ritz hotel or somewhere else fancy. Instead, she was renting a ground-floor room, albeit one with a kitchen, in a house near Primrose Hill which let rooms to actors, and where I, one of those actors, rented the room at the top. I didn't know then that she didn't have money to spare.

I was drawn to her soon after we first met when she asked if she could borrow a shirt because her own was in the laundry. Then, a day or so later, when she asked if I could lend her five pounds until she could get to a bank, we became friends.

In those early days, on my way to my 'between acting jobs', I'd notice her as I was either entering or leaving the house and she'd ask questions if we met in the hall. Where could she mail a letter? Where could she catch a bus to Huston station (she meant Euston station but she never did get that one sorted out). Where did I buy my kebab?

Within a week we were eating kebabs together at Andy's Kebab House or having dinner at Mustoe Bistro in Regents Park Road. Nobody paid her any attention. She didn't dress up or look glamorous. It didn't feel like I was hanging out with a film star at all.

On one of her days off from rehearsal, when I offered to show her the neighbourhood, we walked together over Primrose Hill and then on to Camden Town and I plucked up the courage to ask her about Hollywood. No go. Gloria would say very little. She wanted to know more about me. How come I started acting ten years ago? How long had I spent at drama school? What character was I playing in the television series *Spearhead*, which was about to be aired on British TV?

Watching Gloria figure out cooking one night down in her rooms I saw that she had a copy of *The Complete Works of William Shakespeare* on her desk, which seemed a bit surprising, and so I just mentioned, because I thought she'd be interested, that three years earlier I'd played Romeo in *Romeo and Juliet* at the Crucible Theatre in Sheffield.

Gloria instantly gave up on her cooking. She turned off the grill. She left the bread in the toaster. She put the cheese aside.

Then, sitting down beside me, knowing it by heart, the role she'd always wished she'd played, Gloria recited whole Juliet speeches without fluffing a line.

That long and special night, Gloria told stories about her early stage-work before she went to Metro-Goldwyn-Mayer, and about her lifelong acting teacher – her Scottish mother, Jeannie McDougall – who'd encouraged her passion. Of how Jeannie had been an actress in London in the 1910s and had trained at the prestigious Sir Frank Benson theatre company, an early training ground for actors, which was dedicated to the plays of William Shakespeare and the importance of clear diction and speech. And of how, years later, after Jeannie had married Michael Hallward and they'd left England for America, where Gloria was born, Jeannie subsequently (after divorcing Michael) started her own acting school in California, based entirely on Sir Frank Benson's principles – Shakespeare, diction, speech – and so, in time, Gloria became her pupil.

Knowing so much about Shakespeare's heroines, from Juliet to Rosalind, Gloria told me that when she'd be working on film roles, she and her mother would look for similarities in the character she was playing with some of those heroines from Shakespeare's plays. Is there a hint of Hermia in *Oklahoma*'s Ado Annie, perhaps? Or a layer of Lady Macbeth in Vicki Crawford in *Human Desire*, I've since wondered?

And watching Gloria's films again now, I can detect her mother's insistence in the production of clear diction and speech, particularly in *The Bad and the Beautiful*, where in the first scenes Gloria invests Rosemary Bartlett with perfect enunciation until, in the later scenes, Gloria seems to forget about it and relaxes into her regular, more comfortable speech patterns.

In that spring and summer of 1978, Gloria enjoyed living the kind of life I usually led. We went on walks around London, saw plays at fringe theatres, and, even though Gloria rarely drank alcohol, her favourite tipple being cold milk, she liked to spend evenings together in the local pubs.

Gloria was fascinated by the Plantagenet and Tudor English kings – an American-in-London kind of thing, I supposed then – and so I trooped with her to see Hampton Court Palace and the Tower of London. How excited she would have been if she'd have known then what I learnt, six years after she had died, when I received a letter from Charles Kidd, editor of *Debrett's Peerage*, telling me that while researching his book, *Debrett's Goes to Hollywood*, he'd discovered that Gloria Grahame was a descendent of John of Gaunt, Duke of Lancaster, the son of King Edward the Third.

The place she wanted to visit most though was my hometown of Liverpool. She loved stories about my growing-up there with my eight older brothers and sisters. Her favourite story was one about the Pivvy, an old variety theatre near to where we lived, where my mother was a cleaner. Aged seven, I would accompany her there when she went to do the 'pick up', which involved picking up discarded theatre tickets and sweet wrappers off the floor between shows, and I would go onto the stage as it was being brushed and imagine I was an actor in a play. The first time Gloria did visit my family there, she claimed that Liverpool was the most romantic place on earth. Liverpool? Was she kidding? No. Living back in the city now, thirty years later, I think that Gloria was right.

Having been probed about the relationship over the years, it's even plainer to me now why Gloria and I made the transition from friends to lovers. It happened because we had become intriguingly attracted to each other and had grown increasingly close. There was no song or dance about it. Yes, Gloria was almost thirty years older than me but I'd grown up around sisters twenty years my senior and so I was comfortable around women much older than myself. Yes, my sexuality was fluid, but there were no heavy 'gay or straight' conversations because there was no need. To Gloria and myself, there were no obstacles. It was only as far as other people were concerned that the relationship we shared didn't fit into a box. There were cynics. It was 1978. Eyebrows were raised in a way that perhaps they would not be now. Since then, attitudes towards sexual identity, as well as attitudes towards women, particularly over the age of fifty, have changed enormously. I'm very glad about that.

Having re-read *Film Stars* I'm reminded of how the late 1970s were interesting years for my acting career too. Since being noticed at The National Youth Theatre and then leaving drama school, I'd worked with theatre companies in Glasgow, Sheffield, and London. I'd played Harry in the film *The Comeback*, the lead role in a John Bowen play and the lead role in a three-part series, both for the BBC. Then from July 1978 until July 1981, throughout the entire course of my relationship with Gloria, I was playing Terry Adams in the television drama series *Spearhead*, appearing in sixteen hour-long episodes in all. Gloria was delighted to learn that I was soon to play Trinculo in Derek Jarman's film version of Shakespeare's *The Tempest*, and even more excited to be able to pass on the news to 'Mother'.

When the play *Rain* finished at Watford, Gloria stayed on in London after being offered the role of Lily in the play *A Tribute to Lily Lamont*, which was to be presented at The New End Theatre in Hampstead. She played parts on British television in the autumn of that year and, taking her by surprise, there was renewed film interest in her from both sides of the Atlantic. Gloria was interviewed on radio and there were articles about her in the London press. The British film and theatre world responded and, although Gloria preferred to keep herself out of any limelight, there were invitations for her to give talks at film schools, and to go to film festivals as well as being invited to other special events. Her career was in new bloom. Our personal and private relationship gave confidence to us both. There seemed to be an exciting future ahead.

Over the following two years there were weekends together in Brighton, Glasgow, and Wales. We holidayed on a Greek island where we rented a room from a local who met tourists at the port. Between gaps in recording each season of my television series, and Gloria's shooting schedules for the films *Chilly Scenes in Winter* and *Melvin and Howard*, which took her back to the United States, I visited her at the caravan she owned near a beach in Los Angeles, and I also stayed with her several times at her rented apartment in Hell's Kitchen, New York.

Thinking back now on the course of our relationship I can see clearly when, but not knowing at the time why, it started to change.

It was 1980. It was summer. The telephone woke me at five a.m. It was Gloria calling me from America. The conversation, as usual, was chatty and close and by the end of it we'd worked out that I would travel to see her. Excited by the spur of the moment arrangement, I bought a cheap standby ticket and flew out of London the following day. A scary lightning storm, flashing across a black sky, thundered the sides of my plane as it descended over New York.

It wasn't a surprise to me that Gloria was feeling so tired. From the beginning of the year she'd been determined to do as much work in the theatre as she possibly could and stubbornly pursued roles she'd always wanted to play. Learning and preparing some hefty parts such as Amanda in *Private Lives* and, achieving one of her ambitions, the role of Lady Macbeth; she'd travelled to little-known theatres in faraway places to act in small-scale productions which played for little more than a week. In between plays she'd flown to London and back again twice and she'd been on location in Georgia to film *Mr Griffin and Me*. And it was only the month of July!

The city was humid and hot. Gloria was restless and contrary. She didn't want to stay in and she didn't want to go out. It was only when she was contacted by the Inland Revenue Service to question her over expenses for theatre tickets she'd sent them without providing receipts that she found a renewed energy. Her contrariness turned into crusade.

Over the following days, every evening after dark, I walked with her through the theatre district to pick discarded ticket stubs up from the gutter, as well as any other receipt she thought might satisfy the IRS. How was I to know, twenty-two years earlier, aged seven, and following after my mother picking theatre tickets up from the floor at the theatre in Liverpool, that one day I would be doing exactly the same thing with a film star on the streets of New York?

Hot July turned into hotter August. Gloria became increasingly unsettled. She didn't like her hair or she didn't like her clothes. There were telephone calls. She spent time alone in her room. She dismissed all my concerns. She'd be snappy or short. We'd argue. I took myself walking through the city. There was something not being said. Maybe the relationship was over. There was a secret Gloria was keeping from me. I knew it was time to go home.

I didn't know then that the secret was the sudden return of a cancer she'd never told me about and which she would die from the following year.

My *Spearhead* job took me away filming to Hong Kong at the end of that year and I didn't see Gloria again until those last days in Liverpool. There was a letter she'd sent in which a particular line stood out:

Both Sartre and Camus wrote, that in this life, when we
die, it's only love that is important.

Maybe the fact that my relationship with Gloria was not considered to be legitimate while she was alive was the reason it was hardly acknowledged after she had died. It was only many years later, when I returned to California, that I went with friends to Oakwood Cemetery and I stood at Gloria's grave.

I disengaged from my acting career at about the same time that it disengaged from me. It didn't matter. I went to work in a junk shop at the far end of the Portobello Road. One day a 1950s desk I liked the look of was brought in to be put up for sale, so I bought it for myself. Months later I found an old Hermes typewriter to put on it. Waking up too early one morning, I looked at the typewriter, sat at the desk, and started to write my book.

Not having written anything previously, I didn't have high expectations for the book and thought of it as just my very own story, but when Michael Billington, an actor friend from my *Spearhead* days, read it, he encouraged me to think of it as something more. I sent it to several literary agents but one by one they sent the manuscript back. In a last-ditch attempt, not realizing I'd kept the best till the last, I sent it to Deborah Rogers. Months later, Deborah telephoned to say that she liked it and that she'd given it to Carmen Callil, the managing director of the publishers Chatto and Windus. *Film Stars Don't Die in Liverpool* was published eleven months later, in 1986.

When the book was published it gathered interest from the film world and, after many challenges and a walk down a very long road, it now looks as if a film is to be made by producers Barbara Broccoli and Colin Vaines for Eon Productions, with a screenplay by Matt Greenhalgh and with Paul McGuigan to direct.

I'm indebted to Mathew Turner (no relation) at Rogers, Coleridge and White for taking *Film Stars* up again after all these years, and I'm especially grateful to Georgina Morley at Pan Macmillan for taking a chance on me by re-publishing it.